SCARS EXILE & VINDICATION

Coach Biley,
 Thank you for being such a powerful & positive influence in my life. Your words of encouragement are greatly appreciated.

C.T.I.
July 2012

SCARS EXILE & VINDICATION

My Life As An Experiment

Charles Thomas Jr.

TATE PUBLISHING
AND ENTERPRISES, LLC

Scars, Exile, and Vindication
Copyright © 2012 by Charles Thomas Jr. All rights reserved.

No part of this publication may be reproduced, stored in a retrieval system or transmitted in any way by any means, electronic, mechanical, photocopy, recording or otherwise without the prior permission of the author except as provided by USA copyright law.

This book is designed to provide accurate and authoritative information with regard to the subject matter covered. This information is given with the understanding that neither the author nor Tate Publishing, LLC is engaged in rendering legal, professional advice. Since the details of your situation are fact dependent, you should additionally seek the services of a competent professional.

The opinions expressed by the author are not necessarily those of Tate Publishing, LLC.

Published by Tate Publishing & Enterprises, LLC
127 E. Trade Center Terrace | Mustang, Oklahoma 73064 USA
1.888.361.9473 | www.tatepublishing.com

Tate Publishing is committed to excellence in the publishing industry. The company reflects the philosophy established by the founders, based on Psalm 68:11,
"The Lord gave the word and great was the company of those who published it."

Book design copyright © 2012 by Tate Publishing, LLC. All rights reserved.
Cover design by Erin DeMoss
Interior design by Sarah Kirchen

Published in the United States of America
ISBN: 978-1-61862-366-9
1. Biography & Autobiography / Personal Memoirs
2. Biography & Autobiography / General
12.06.11

DEDICATION

I dedicate this book to all the people out there who are struggling to survive. I dedicate this book to anyone out there who has faced some level of adversity and had the resiliency to move forward despite the circumstances and odds against them. I dedicate this book to those who understand the power of faith and are awe-inspired by the omnipotence, omnipresence, and omniscience of the Creator. I dedicate this book to all people who live and let live, who are not quick to judge, who show empathy and compassion, and who strive to make their corner of the world a better place.

ACKNOWLEDGEMENTS

First and foremost, I would like to thank my mother, father, and sister for the unconditional love, support, understanding, and guidance that they have so graciously bestowed upon me over the years. The confidence that they and other members of my family (cousins, aunts, and uncles) have consistently placed in me is most appreciated, and I would like to extend my sincerest gratitude. While this book goes into in-depth levels of detail regarding my upbringing, familial relationships, and associated interactions, any negative feelings that were once held in my heart and mind no longer remain. I have forgiven anyone who committed what I perceived to be any indiscretions against me, and I hope they have forgiven me for anything I may have done to offend them.

I would like to extend thanks to the Notre Dame family, the UTSA Roadrunner family, and the Creighton BlueJay family. The experiences I gained at these institutions of higher learning as well as the relationships I developed with an assortment of wonderful people will be forever cherished. Additionally, I would like to say thanks and extend my utmost gratitude to a host of friends: Akil, Darnell, Ed, Nelson, Torrian, Toya, Amanda, Monique, PJ, Alesha, Josh. Y'all make me want to do better, be better, and live better. For those of you that I did not mention, I love you the same. Thank you for being a part of my life and allowing me to learn from you.

Finally, to my loving wife and baby girl, Manthanee and Masani, thank you for being there. I thank God everyday for allowing me to be a part of your lives. The love, support, and care the two of you exhibit daily are greatly appreciated. As we live, we grow. As we grow, we love. As we love, we become one.

TABLE OF CONTENTS

Preface 11

Divinely Inspired 15

The Informative Years 23

Do Not Take It Personal 35

Visualize and It Will Materialize 55

Learn to Fly 89

Focus: The Sharper It Is, the Sharper You Are 103

The Breakup 121

Downward Spiral 137

Resilience: Bounce Back 161

Help from All the Wrong, But Right, Places 171

Faith, Desire, Patience 187

God Favors the Faithful 209

The Prophecy 213

PREFACE

The day began as usual. I woke up and thanked God for allowing me to see another day because I was surely undeserving of such grace and mercy. It was summer time, so the basketball court was my sanctuary. My job was to get better so that I could be the star that, in my mind, I was destined to be. There was nothing strange to the start of this particular day, and the sad thing was that the ending was just the same—nothing out of the ordinary. Every day, after leaving the gym, I would walk down the street to clear my head and relax before going home. I wanted to go to college, but I was not sure where. The walks after workouts were quite helpful. This day, as I was walking down the street dribbling a basketball, I saw two shoes behind a dumpster. Ordinarily, I would have not even given those shoes a second look; but these shoes were red, and they were not supposed to be.

I cautiously walked up to the dumpster, looked behind it and, lo and behold, a young man lay there, his body riddled with bullets, and his blood everywhere. Did I panic? No. I had seen death before and heard about it so much that I was no longer afraid of it. This day, though, I felt sad. What had he done to have been so savagely murdered and left behind a dumpster? Where were his parents? Did he have kids? Did anyone even know he was missing? That sight solidified in my mind that I would never be a victim of my circumstances. You want to know what is so bad about this situation? I did not stay there for long. I continued to dribble my ball down the street and thought to myself, *I wonder what Mom has cooked.* By the time I finished my routine and was walking back toward my car, the cops had shown up. At least he was not out there by himself for too long. Who knows how his loved ones reacted upon hearing such tragic news. All I know is that at that moment, I decided that I needed to get away from such violence. I did not know how I was going to do it, but I knew why I wanted to do it. I was seventeen years old, and the decision was made. Being a lost soul was not an option. I wanted to make a way, even if the world said there was no way.

Viktor Frankl, in *Man's Search for Meaning,* approvingly quotes the words of Nietzsche when he says, "He who has a why to live for can bear almost any how." I understand *why* I live and, as a result, dealing with the *how* is only secondary. The pain that will come through in this book is real; but in order for me to release and finally understand why I went through what I have gone through, I had to write about it. Talking about it was not helpful, and reading about the lives and stories of others was not enough. Trying to make sense out of something I did not and will probably never understand kept me up on several occasions. Many nights I would sit in my room contemplating, wondering, pondering, and asking why. Was I ever able to come up with a logical answer? The answer is no. Many nights I would cry and ask God, "Why me?" Then I began to realize that God only tests those whom He knows can handle it. I began to understand that the trials and tribulations that I faced on an almost daily basis meant that God was watching me. He thought so much of me and believed so much in the product that He made that He saw it fit to test me. I gained solace and an indescribable level of comfort when I went to the Bible for answers and learned that one of God's very own children, Job, even asked why. I learned that asking *why* is not wrong as long as faith is not lost. Just as Job was restored, I, too, will receive God's grace and mercy.

As I write this, I cry and still wonder why I put myself through so much senseless pain. I guess it is because no one else will listen. Maybe they don't care, but more than likely, the real answer is they don't understand. I have been a mystery to many people throughout my short existence on this planet. Some think they have figured me out, while others have given up. Am I an enigma? Have I been sent to this earth by the Creator to challenge the very being and thought processes of others? Am I an inspiration to others? Was I made to be a comet in a planet full of stars? Is it my obligation to motivate others? Is it my duty to give other people a reason to believe, a sense of hope? Why do I ask so many questions and try to understand such complex issues? I do not know the answer to many of these questions. What I do know, however, is that writing my story was therapeutic. It gave me a deeper meaning into what this world has in store for all of us, and it gave me the opportunity to enrich lives and hopefully be a blessing to others.

Writing my story is also meant to be inspirational for those who fight earthly battles on a daily basis. We are all inspired by those individuals who have physical deformities and rise above the crowd to make a way out of no way, but what about those of us who only have scars on the inside? We need to encourage others as well and reiterate that everything will turn out just fine in the end. Many young black men usually only hear about the successes of other black men after they have made it. We now know that Jay-Z had a "hard knock life," but we did not know it until his music made him famous. We now know that Chris Gardner was once homeless before opening his own finance and investment firm and becoming a self-made multi-millionaire. We found out, after the fact, that Tyler Perry was living in his car writing plays and never losing his faith in God. They give us anecdotes about how they made it; but we were not there to participate in their struggles.

I write this book and tell my story as a young man who is currently swimming against the current with no life raft just like many other young men and women. I want them to know that they are not alone. I want to give them hope and a reason to believe. I want them to know that there is never a reason to run alone. I want them to be there with me, and I want to be there with them as we swim against the current and do our best to keep our heads above water, not succumbing to the raging waters that are trying so desperately to drown us. I want them to know that it is okay to show their scars. Scars heal and are a true indication that you handled adversity and got over it. Scars remind us that the past is real and give us motivation to move forward into the future with an attitude of optimism and a promise of better days to come.

"Enlightened," "enriched," "blessed," and "peaceful" are only a few of the words that come to mind. It is not often that a man can come to grips with his past and release it so that it does not hold his future hostage. Harold Kushner said it best when he wrote, "Forces beyond your own control can take away everything you possess except one thing: your freedom to choose how you will respond to the situation. You cannot control what happens to you in life, but you can always control what you will feel and do about what happens to you."

While I have not made sense out of many of the things that have happened to me, I understand that everything is not meant for me to understand. Sometimes if you do not see it, it was not meant for you to see; and if you were not born with it, it was not meant for you to be. I do know, however, that what God has for you, no one can take from you, and whomsoever God guides, no one can lead astray. I also realize and recognize that every storm that I encountered, every mountain that I climbed, every battle that I fought and won, were all part of God's divine plan to make me a better person—a leader, a follower, a man amongst boys and, most importantly, a son of the King.

DIVINELY INSPIRED

In the beginning, God created the heavens and earth. In seven days, He created the world as we know it and everything in it. He created flowers, birds, wildlife, mountain ranges, oceans—the list is exhaustive. Above all, in His infinite wisdom and omnipotence, He saw fit to create humanity. As a result, I am a true reflection of God's own heart, and I know that I am divinely inspired. Proverbs 3:5-6 says, "Trust in the Lord with all your heart and lean not unto your own understanding. In all your ways acknowledge Him, and He will direct your paths." I have it tattooed on my right arm, and I say it and live by it daily. It is what inspires me to continually take on new challenges and gives me the courage to say, even in the midst of a storm, "Do your worst." Because I have a divine inspiration and am blessed and highly favored by God, I recognize the importance of that Bible verse. Some people have asked me how it is possible that I have done so well for myself at such a young age. My response to them is that I walk a higher path because I serve a higher power. My advice to you is to find something that has meaning in your life, something that you are passionate about, something that you have no fear in discussing and/or teaching, and know that if your inspiration comes from above, failure is not an option.

What does it mean to be truly divinely inspired? There is not a Merriam-Webster definition, and each person may have his or her own thoughts about what it means to be divinely inspired. Since I am not a mind reader and do not have extrasensory perception, I cannot comment on what others may think, feel, or believe. All I can tell you is what it means to me. To be divinely inspired means that in everything you do, you do it for the glory of God and for the betterment of His kingdom on earth and above. It means doing the right thing when no one is watching. It means being sincere in your dealings with others. It means helping an old woman or man across the street. It means giving someone your time, even if you are busy. It means treating people as you want to be treated. It means knowing that God has a plan for your life, and He will not lead you astray. To be divinely inspired means that you are more than willing to listen to the problems of others, take the cross from their shoulders, remove their burdens, and give them a reason to believe. It means you show compassion and empathy for others. It means you are humble in your dealings with others. It means that no matter what the situation may be, you know that with God on your side, you can handle it.

We all get our inspiration from somewhere. Some people get inspiration from relatives or friends, some from professional athletes and entertainers, while others receive their inspiration from individuals who tell the rags to riches story. While all of those types of inspiration are logical and give our lives meaning, the best form of inspiration that anyone—man, woman, boy, or girl—can receive is divine inspiration. It never steers you wrong; and you always know that even if you veer off the path for a while, one way or another, you will find your way back home.

All too often young men, black or white, feel that their inspiration comes from something other than God. They see the rappers and entertainers on TV glorifying the gangsta life when they talk about money, drugs, fame, or fortune. They fail to realize that many, if not all, of these rappers have an unshakeable faith in God. I smile during every award show when an individual gets up to speak and the first thing said is, "I would like to thank God, without whom none of this would be possible." They couldn't have given a stronger opening statement. That sentence instills the belief it states into youthful minds.

I am a huge hip-hop fan and believe that these individuals have the power to change the world as we see it. Sean "Diddy" Combs was able to single-handedly change the way blacks view the voting process; "Vote or Die" was his slogan. Not only did his slogan catch on, it spread like wildfire. T-shirts with the phrase were bought and worn, and people had it written on their shoes. I even saw one kid on *106th & Park* who had the barber shave it on the back of his head.

Although Diddy and every other human being have free will, his actions were not done without forethought and positive intent. He was divinely inspired.

Tupac Shakur, my personal favorite rapper of all time, was also divinely inspired. People from all walks of life listened to and loved his work. If his inspiration was not divine, I would be at a loss for words. The American public saw the "thug life" side of the man, but they did not really understand his pains. Do not let my last statement move you from my point. I am not here to discuss Tupac's character, his life, his movies, his lyrics, or his actions on or off camera. I am talking about his inspiration. Take the following lyrical content, for example:

> Come listen to my truest thoughts, my truest feelings, all my peers doing years beyond drug dealing. How many caskets can we witness before we see it's hard to live this life without God, so we must ask forgiveness…

There have been many things said to date about 2Pac, but one thing that can never be said is that his music did not come from the heart and it was not divinely inspired.

What about non hip-hop artists? you ask. There are countless numbers of individuals who have been divinely inspired, and their successes and contributions to the world will not go unnoticed. Oprah Winfrey, Barack Obama, Chris Gardner, Eddie

Robinson, and Dr. Ben Carson are just a few of the thousands, maybe even millions, of people in the world whose inspiration is divine. Each person has paved the way for others, and the journey has not been easy. Did they take the path of least resistance or the road less traveled? I would say, "No."

Each of the aforementioned individuals was, at one point or another, in a position in which giving up would have been the easiest choice they could have made. After climbing the mountains they climbed, jumping over the hurdles they jumped, weathering the storms they weathered, and fighting the battles they fought, turning back was not an option. Confucius once said, "Our greatest glory is not in never falling, but in rising every time we fall." Without divine inspiration, living a life based on that premise is futile at best. The level of distress, angst, worry, anxiety, and pure fear that can overcome an individual in trying times is often too much to bear. Not for me, though. Not for the people I just mentioned. Why? Because our inspiration is divine and fighting is all we know.

Oprah Winfrey is a woman of God's own heart. A child of unmarried teenage parents and the victim of sexual molestation, she could have easily thrown in the towel, but she didn't. She persevered and found her own happiness. She knew that her ability, or lack thereof, to make a difference in this world rested solely on her shoulders. She knew that with God on her side, she would be able to accomplish any task that she set out to achieve, and accomplish she did. Oprah Winfrey is an American multiple Emmy Award-winning host of *The Oprah Winfrey Show*, the highest rated talk show in the history of television. She is a fabulous book critic, an Academy Award-nominated actress, and a magazine publisher. Oprah has been described as the richest African American in the twenty-first century—a billionaire and the most philanthropic African American of all time. Now that's what I call being divinely inspired.

Barack Obama was also divinely inspired. Based on his story, he didn't have such a rosy upbringing, either. Son of a Kenyan father and a white American mother, Obama was involuntarily placed in the middle of the races. In his memoir, *Dreams of My Father*, Obama describes his experiences growing up in his mother's American middle class family. His father left him at an extremely early age, and he notes that his knowledge pertaining to his father came mainly through family stories and photographs. Of his early childhood, Obama writes, "My father looked nothing like the people around me; he was black as pitch, my mother white as milk."

The book not only describes his intrapersonal struggles as a young adult to reconcile and understand social perceptions of his multiracial heritage, but it also discusses his uses of alcohol, marijuana, and blow during his teenage years. To make matters worse, his mother died from uterine cancer shortly after the publication of *Dreams of My Father*. Did he have a reason to give up and live the life that many people assume that young black men with underprivileged upbringings will lead? *Absolutely!*

However, he acted in diametric opposition of how people assumed and maybe even expected that he would act. His inspiration was divine, and he went against the grain. He wanted to prove to himself and to others that regardless of current circumstances, things can change—and change for the better.

Because of Barack Obama's divine inspiration, he went to Columbia University, where he majored in political science with a concentration in international relations and he received his BA degree. After undergrad, Obama worked for a few years then decided to enter Harvard law school. He completed his JD degree magna cum laude. Now the man who had a difficult childhood holds the highest office in the land, president of the United States of America. When your inspiration is divine, the sky is truly the limit. Can you do it? Yes, you can.

Chris Gardner, the character portrayed by Will Smith in the movie *The Pursuit of Happyness,* credits his tenacity and success to his "spiritual genetics." Mr. Gardner is also a man who could have chosen a life of crime and violence as a result of being a product of such a world. Fortunately, he was divinely inspired. He had few positive role models in his life. His biological father lived in another state, and his stepfather was violent. Gardner has been noted as saying that God and his mother were his sources of inspiration and strength. His mother encouraged him to believe in himself, and she instilled in him the concept of self-reliance and self-confidence. His stepfather's violent outbursts and vicious attacks oftentimes left his mother badly beaten and nearly fatally injured. His mother was imprisoned when she was reported to authorities for working while collecting welfare. As a result, Gardner and his siblings were raised in foster care during her incarceration. The children were put into foster care once again when Gardner's mother attempted to burn down the house while her abusive partner was inside.

Because of the horrific sequence of events that Gardner had to constantly witness, he knew he wanted better. Having such a high level of cerebral capacity, Gardner determined that alcoholism, domestic abuse, child abuse, illiteracy, fear, and powerlessness were all things that he did not want to associate with on any level.

Despite his best efforts, Gardner became homeless and had the responsibility of caring for his son. Unbelievable. To have the courage, strength, determination, and intestinal fortitude to not give up when all hope is gone is a testament to his will. Gardner not only made his way out of the depths of hell, but he did it with class, poise, and gracefulness. A self-made multimillionaire, entrepreneur, motivational speaker, published author, and philanthropist, Gardner became the CEO of his own stock brokerage firm, Gardner Rich. I consider that divine inspiration at its best.

Dr. Ben Carson has been quoted as saying, "Never get too big for God. Never drop God out of your life." Dr. Carson was an inner city kid from Detroit with poor grades and little motivation. He had a mother who married at the age of thirteen and had a third-grade education. Despite the cards being stacked against him, he had a divine inspiration and a very strong and wise mother. Dr. Carson's mother had a strong desire for her sons to succeed, instilling in them the omnipotence and omnipresence of God and pressuring her sons to go from the bottom of the class to the top. Dr. Carson had no reason to strive for excellence the way that he did other than his sources of inspiration. His mother saw a special gift in him and believed in him and his abilities so much that he had no choice but to begin to believe in himself, and believe and achieve he did. Carson graduated from Yale University with a BA in psychology and earned his medical degree from the University of Michigan.

In 1987, Dr. Carson gained worldwide recognition for his part in the first successful separation of Siamese twins joined at the back of the head. The surgery was extremely complex and delicate. It took five months of planning and twenty-two hours of actual surgery involving a surgical plan that Carson helped initiate. Carson has received numerous honors and awards, including more than twenty honorary doctorate degrees. Carson was also appointed to the President's Council on Bioethics by George W. Bush in 2004. Dr. Carson is a testimony to what it means to be divinely inspired. In being a man graced with such human attributes as humility, courage, compassion, decency, intelligence, and sensitivity, he serves as a role model for people from all walks of life. He gives people a reason to believe and a reason to dream that they can attempt the impossible and actually accomplish it. His sources of inspiration give us all a reason to know and believe wholeheartedly that being divinely inspired means impossible is nothing.

I have discussed, on the periphery, individuals that have given me hope and a reason to believe. Each person could have enumerated a myriad of unavoidable life circumstances that caused him or her to lose the faith, give up, and not follow his or her heart. They had something that many people search for their entire lives and never find—divine inspiration. They recognize that all the "shoulda," "woulda", "couldas" in the world can never make up for one "I did." Each person had an unwavering faith in God and because they did it, I know I can do it. Because of their stories, I know that although life may be hard and things may sometimes not go my way, I understand how critically important it is to never cry when the sun is gone, because the tears will not allow me to see the stars. A friend once told me that people who are divinely inspired and emotionally committed to something behave in ways that defy logic and often produce results that are well beyond expectations. They pursue impossible dreams, work ridiculous hours, and resolve unsolvable problems. *Who am I?* you ask. I am the seed who doesn't need much to succeed. I am a son of the King, God's greatest miracle, a testament of His creation, a reflection of His own heart. I am living proof that dreams come true. I am divinely inspired.

THE INFORMATIVE YEARS

The early years of a child's life are supposed to be fun, memorable, enjoyable, and shape the way we think, respond, and act in predictable and uncertain situations. These years, ages zero to fourteen are, in my eyes, best suited for observation, emulation, and overall information gathering. These are the times when we are supposed to look to our parents and other adult figures in an effort to decipher right from wrong, good from bad, fact from fiction, love from lust, appropriate from inappropriate, etc. These are the times when we learn to model certain types of behaviors and gain a deeper understanding of our talents. We begin to figure out what talents are God-given and what talents we need to work on in order to not only meet but exceed expectations.

During the informative years, we as young men are supposed to rely on the guidance from our fathers, older brothers, uncles, and other close male associates in order to accurately conceptualize and recognize the nuances and intricacies involved with being a man. We are supposed to learn how to treat women with respect; how to love our children unconditionally; and how to balance home, life, and work in order to meet the needs of the family. We are supposed to learn the essence of hard work, what it means and how to be a God-fearing man, and what it takes to not only survive, but also excel in this world.

From women—our mothers, sisters, aunts, and older female associates—we are supposed to learn how to efficiently and effectively handle conflict, how to treat a woman, how to love our family and friends, how to cook, how to wash clothes, how to be self-sufficient, etc. We are supposed to learn how to deal with the bad as well as the good, how to react in a crisis, and how to maintain a high level of composure when things do not go as planned. Notice I said "supposed to learn." For me, this was not necessarily the case.

Although I was raised in a dual-parent household and my parents managed to not get a divorce, our family was what modern day psychologists and psychiatrists like to call "dysfunctional." Don't get me wrong; Mom and Dad were great. I look up to them like I have never looked up to anyone else before in my life. They made unbelievable and selfless sacrifices, hard choices, and did everything in their power to make me and my younger sister comfortable. There was not anything that we needed that they did not struggle to get for us so that we would feel special. That being said, there were many mistakes that were made that have had a negative impact on me and those who grew up around me. Because of that, I have a better understanding of what to do and what not to do when I become a husband and enter fatherhood.

The informative years, ages zero to fourteen are, in my mind, spotty at best. These memories fade in and out, not because I have a bad memory or I was too young to remember, but because I have subconsciously tried to repress them. I feel myself getting weaker as I think about those years, and I get even madder when I actually write about them. My childhood, although from an external viewpoint may have been filled with love and adoration, clothes, shoes, basketball courts, trampolines, private school educations and the like, was much more than what those on the outside looking in saw. It was marred with emotional abuse, domestic violence, physical abuse, and sometimes a lack of support.

My father had other daughters from a previous marriage, and me and my younger sister never got the chance to really know them. I know they are my sisters, but deep down I feel as if they never really considered me their brother. I do not think it was done intentionally, but they were never given the option to really know my younger sister or me. Our family dynamic was the classic family movie in which kids were the products of two different relationships. There was always a rift between the families. Although I was not absolutely clear as to what was actually taking place, I knew something was wrong. They did not come to my house much, I didn't go to their house much, and when we did see each other, there was always some level of arguing. I never really cared too much about getting attention, I don't think, but I do remember getting upset when my younger sister got upset or something negative was said to my mother. I just wanted to play basketball and have fun. I never asked for much, but I was often the victim of painful punishments. I have gone through twenty-nine years on this planet, and I have only regretted two things. The first is not knowing my sisters better, and the second will be discussed in a later chapter. Even that, however, was a learning experience. Not knowing my sisters, though, has really bothered me. Anyway, back to the informative years.

As previously mentioned, these years were marred with conflict, controversy, and some level of physical and/or mental abuse. My father is a wonderful man now, but when I was a baby, I would have to say otherwise. He was controlling, aggressive, violent, domineering, charming, funny, smooth, and deceptive. He was made up of the perfect ingredients to trick the outside world. It has been said that the greatest trick the devil ever pulled was convincing the world that he did not exist. While my father never attempted to convince humanity that he was a mere illusion, a figment of the imagination, he did an extremely impressive job of masking his true self. He was Batman during the day, Freddie Kruger at night. I was told as child that when I was born, he did not claim me. He said I was not his. Can you imagine the impact that has on a small boy when he hears such statements over and over and over again? If you can, I am sorry that you had to endure the same traumatic experiences that I had to endure. But understand that if you did experience the same unfortunate chain of events, you are a better person because of it. You are a product of your environment, and you should not be afraid or ashamed of the wonderful, God-fearing, respectful person that you have become. It could be worse.

I remember, even as a little boy, him hitting my mother or screaming at her for no reason. Anything could have triggered his tirade: asking a question the wrong way, asking too many questions, not answering how he wanted her to answer, taking too long to answer. In fact, it did not even have to be that. He could have just had a bad day at work and decided she would be the object of his aggression. I can only imagine how much of a helpless feeling it was when one of my older sisters saw my mom getting hit with a water hose and not have the power, knowledge, and/or resources to do anything about it. I was not alive when that incident occurred—only told about it. To not know, especially as a small child, what was going to happen to Mom and why she was in the current situation was terrifying, to say the least. Thinking about it now brings back the same helpless feelings, except now I know that it will never happen again.

I remember him hitting her. I remember the look in his eyes. I can remember him talking to her like she was a child and deserving of her punishment. I can remember him leaving after it was over and then her just hugging me in an effort to reassure her only son that no matter what happened, everything was going to be all right. I remember wondering, *Where is daddy? Why is he never home?* No real explanations were given; but as I got older, I started to interpret different situations and extrapolate my own conclusions. It was not her fault. It was not my fault or the fault of the girls. Dad was his own man, and he let outside forces negatively influence his decision-making abilities. I cannot say with 100 percent certainty that his friends were beating their wives as well, but I am pretty sure some of them had to be. There was talk, more than likely, of what instruments to use to leave the least amount of visible bruising, or what statements to make to cause an immediate argument so that violence was the next logical choice. How he, or any other man for that matter, can hit a woman is beyond my comprehension, but it happened.

It was a cold autumn night, and I could not have been any more than three years old because I do not remember my youngest sister being born. An innocent baby caught in the crossfire. All I know is that I was scared of what was going on inside of my house, and I had to go and get help. Dad was in one of his moods again and Mom, being mom, wasn't ever going to back down. I remember hearing yelling and screaming and did not know what to do. To diffuse the inevitability of more violence, I ran out of the house to go next door and get help. To show you how rage can mentally incapacitate a person beyond belief, my dad actually tried to close the garage on me. His only son—a baby. I had to slide under the door to go and get help. I ran next door screaming, "Mommy and Daddy are fighting again." Help had arrived. They went next door, de-escalated the situation, and order in my world was restored... at least for a little while.

That was the last time I remember mom and dad physically fighting each other. There could have been more violent outbursts but, like I said, my memory of this period is quite sporadic. I also think this was the last time they had a physical confrontation because my baby sister was born shortly thereafter, and Mom filed for divorce because getting beat again was no longer an option. I am not sure what was said and by whom to talk her out of it, but they have been married for thirty-plus years. Can't live with him, can't live without him. Can't live with her, can't live without her. Guess that was their motto... who knows.

After my father stopped physically abusing my mother, I became the object of his physical aggression and emotional abuse. I can recall being screamed at and whooped for no apparent reason. Well, in his eyes, he had a reason. The girls, all of them, even at a young age, were conniving, manipulative, and sneaky. They would make up stories or say that I did things because they knew

I would get into trouble. There were times when one of them would change the TV channel and then when Dad asked who did it, they would point to me and I, involuntarily, had to take the blame as well as the punishment.

My youngest sister has been a mastermind for years, an artist of deception, a wolf in sheep's clothing, if you will. She knew just what to say in order to get her way, and she knew exactly how to say it in order for me to get into trouble. By trouble, I mean I got my a** beat with switches, belts, cords—whatever was in close proximity. In his eyes, she could do no wrong; so if there was a complaint of any sort, clearly, I was the culprit. I was in the house, so logically it had to be me, right? Apparently so, because there were never any questions asked, merely consequences and repercussions for offenses that I often did not commit. It is kind of funny to look back on it now, because some of those whoopings I deserved. I was bad as a kid. Not in terms of doing anything illegal, but just bad. I would curse you out, fight you, and do whatever necessary to achieve my desired objective. Therefore, I am not claiming to be an angel in all of this; some of my punishments were warranted. Other times, however, they were not.

I remember we would play fight or wrestle and as long as she was winning, everything was cool. As soon as the tables would turn, bloody murder was my offense. She would run and tell Dad that I hit her too hard, or she would just scream his name. Many times, he just began hitting me and never even considered asking what happened. I was a kid. What was I to do? Was I supposed to say, "Check this out, Pops. I think it's best if we sit down over a donut and some coffee and iron out some of the issues that we seem to be having as father and son. I feel that the situation can be rectified in a more agreeable manner if you would give me the opportunity to express myself and clearly articulate what actually happened"? Sounds good, but that was never an option of mine. More often than not, the conversation went something like this: "What have I told you about messing with that girl? I have told you over and over again to leave her alone, and I am going to beat your a** until you understand what I'm saying." This was all said, by the way, while he was hitting me with the belt. How you oftentimes see it portrayed in the movies is how I experienced it. Comical, but not really.

I would be remiss if I didn't discuss my mom's role in this. Oftentimes, when the whoopings would take place, she would be away from home. She was still working during this period of my life and if she was not at work, she was out getting things for the house to make our lives more comfortable. Usually, if she was home, the whoopings wouldn't be so bad and wouldn't last as long because she would stop them. Sometimes, well actually, quite a bit of the time, she would be the disciplinarian. It was cool, though. Her whoopings would only sting for a little while; they never really hurt me. I was always a tough little kid and my moms isn't that big, so I was good, for the most part. I digress. Dad has always been a tough, no-nonsense kind of guy; but with me, he often took it too far. I remember there were times when I honestly could not sit down comfortably because of the whelps from switches or the mere pain from the belt constantly hitting me.

The worst whooping I ever had happened when I was in the third grade. It was my fault, though. I forged my dad's signature on a parent release form for an elementary school field trip. It was a major mistake and I know that now, but I did not think of the potential consequences when I signed his name to the paper. We have the same name, so being the child prodigy that I was, I figured the teacher wouldn't know the difference. Wrong answer. Not only did she know the difference, but she also pulled the biggest hater move ever and told on a brotha. Why did she do that? I still ask myself that question to this day. Why did I forge his signature is an even better question. I claim youthful ignorance—seems appropriate to me.

The story continues. I came home from school and my dad said, "Hey, son, come in the basement for a minute. I want to holla at you." Now, as I have already explained to you, I am and always have been quite the astute individual. We, as human beings, are creatures of habit, and I began to recognize that at an early age. Dad only went into the basement to bring clean clothes out of the dryer, check the humidifier, or fix a broken light. This day, however, he was sitting on a workout bench. He was not an avid weight lifter, and there were no weights on the rack. At this point, I was in a state of sheer terror. It truly was fear and not just a heightened sense of things. He calmly asked about the consent form and the impending field trip. I pled the fifth; I refused to answer any questions that might incriminate my friends or myself. It was too late because he already knew the answer. The tirade began. Not only were my feelings hurt because my teacher rolled on me, Mom did not help, Dad was mad, there was no time to run, and I also was not allowed to go on the field trip. All of the adults were in agreement to teach me a lesson. I consider this conspiracy theory at its best.

I share this story with you jokingly because this was a whooping that I did not mind. I deserved it. To this day, I get a little bit apprehensive when I have to sign my full name. I always think I am going to make a mistake and put "senior" at the end of it and not "junior." This is a mistake I do not want to make ever again.

During these years, my second mother died. She was my neighbor, but a second mother nonetheless. I really don't remember much about it, but all I know is that she went into the hospital for what I thought was a routine visit, and never came home. Devastated is not even the appropriate word to describe my feelings. I was unable to fathom why God would take her away from me. It was not fair, and I was not at all amused at His choice. When my mother was being unreasonable and would not concede to my requests and demands, I would go next door and get it from her. She was like my own personal genie. If my mother said no, I would go next door, and my wish would be granted. I was sad to see her go but was constantly told that she was in a better place where she would not have to suffer or be in any pain. I accepted her fate and knew that God had it all under control. Although it was not clear to me, I knew the world was unfolding as it should.

Fast forward to about age ten. I know I have skipped some years, but my recollection of those years is faulty. It was at this age that I began to figure out that was I somewhat intelligent and athletic. My mom always told me do the best that I could in everything that I did and, more often than not, my best would be better than the next person's best. I took what she said to heart and have managed to live my whole life by that philosophy. In the fourth grade, my parents sent me to another elementary school. It was here that my competitive nature and desire to be the best really manifested itself. I began to try to do really well in school and began my pursuit of basketball greatness. In addition, this was the period of my life when I began getting into trouble at school.

Let's discuss the good side of me first. I won the citywide spelling bee and was placed in the top ten in the county. I began working on my basketball skills and also began to realize that soccer and track were also sports in which I could excel. The only bad part about the fourth grade was that I couldn't begin playing competitive sports until the fifth grade. It was during this year that my best friend, Lake (well, we call each other cousins now), came to join me in my quest for mischief and sports dominance. Until I met Lake, I was quite sure that there was no one in the galaxy that was even remotely close to my skill level in any sport. My theory was seriously threatened the first week of school when I saw him playing basketball. He was taller, faster, stronger, and could jump higher. I was not impressed and loved challenges. So I challenged him to a game of one-on-one. He won, of course, but that was the beginning of a beautiful friendship.

Most kids would have continued to play one-on-one with negative outcomes until they could not play anymore. I did the polar opposite of that. I figured since he was better than I was, and no one else was better than me, we should just team up and beat everyone two-on-two. And that we did. We never lost one game of two-on-two from the fifth through the eighth grade—and you thought the Celtics were a dynasty. We were like Superman and Batman, willing and ready to take on all repeat challengers and newcomers. Although we were teammates, secretly I worked hard every day to become a better player than he was, and I am sure he was well aware of my intentions. Although those intentions were completely honorable, being second place was not an option. It was not until about the eighth grade that I consistently began to win one-on-one games. I began to win, not because his skill level was diminishing, but because my focus was exemplary. Once I realized that I could win at the small things in life, taking on bigger challenges was inevitable.

Competitive basketball, soccer, and track all began in grade five. My dreams were turning into realities. I was faster than most of the other soccer players, so it was a natural fit for me to play a wing position and have an opportunity to score goals. I played soccer from the fifth through ninth grades and loved every second of it because it taught me all of the intangibles that were needed to succeed in basketball. Coach Roy was probably one of, if not the best, coach I have ever had. First, he gave me the green light to do pretty much whatever I wanted to do on the soccer field but, most importantly, he was motivating, inspirational, helpful, and understanding. He was a teacher, knew that many of us were special talents, and did whatever he could to help us reach our potential. After soccer season was over, basketball began. Happy, excited, amused, giddy, and floating on cloud nine are all words to describe how I felt the day I made the team. Although I was on the B-team that year, I was still nice with it. I was, by far, the smallest kid on the court, but I definitely had the most heart. I had a gladiator-like mentality—fearless.

Grade five was also when I began to realize that athletics and academics were one in the same. My parents always preached education so I knew that if I did not excel scholastically, excelling on the field of competition would not even be an option. As my quest for scholastic excellence began, my strengths and weaknesses became apparent. Reading, writing, and virtually every other subject other than math were my strong suits. Math, on the other hand, was my kryptonite. I am not entirely sure why it was so hard for me to grasp mathematical concepts, but it was. As I look back on it now, I know that it was all mental. Math was hard for me because I constantly told myself that math was hard, that I wasn't good at it, and that I couldn't do it. It was a self-fulfilling prophecy. Thoughts became things. While I told myself I wasn't good at subjects math-related, I recognized that I was good in other areas, such as spelling and reading. As a result, that is where I focused the majority of my attention. Even at a young age, I figured it would be better to focus on my strengths rather than be consumed by my apparent weaknesses.

Recognizing my talents, my fourth grade teacher convinced me to enter a spelling competition. In the beginning, I was very anxious. Some of the words I had never even heard of, so how I would ever be able to spell them was a question I often asked myself. As I began to read and study more in preparation for the competition, those worries evaporated. There was not any word that I didn't think I couldn't spell. At the elementary school level, I was right. I won the spelling bee and spelled every single word I was given correctly. I then went on to place highly in the county spelling bee. After the county spelling bee, competition increased. Unfortunately, I did not win. From that moment on, I knew that I had to be relentless in my pursuit of excellence. Because I love competition so much, I re-entered the spelling bee every year up until the eighth grade and won in the sixth and eighth grades.

While it may seem like everything was going well for me as a young child, the reality of it is that it was not. My parents constantly argued with each other, I was getting into fights with kids in the neighborhood and school, and my dad would oftentimes get mad and whoop me for no reason. We would argue with each other constantly over little things so minute that I do not even remember 95 percent of the disagreements. I just know that they all ended with me getting a whooping or punching a hole through the bathroom door. I was not sure what the future held, but I prayed and knew that better days were to come. High school was next, and I had to prepare for another challenge. Dealing with everything that was going on at home would make everything else seem easy… or so I thought.

DO NOT TAKE IT PERSONAL

Before I get too deep into this chapter and tell you all about academics and athletics, I have to talk about the home life. Through all of the adversity that I had to deal with at school, on the field of competition, and all of the hours spent studying to excel academically, my home life was miserably dysfunctional. There was constant arguing: arguments between me and my dad, arguments between my mom and my dad, spats between me and my little sister, and all-out battles between me, my mom, and my dad. I felt so bad for my baby sister because oftentimes, she was caught in the crossfire. Not knowing why arguments were taking place, she could only sit idly by, wondering why, and many nights she cried.

My dad and I were not as close in high school as we probably should have been, mainly because I did not like the way he treated moms, and he knew that I was diametrically opposed to his actions as a father and husband. I would sometimes come home from school, and he would just bug out for no reason. He yelled, screamed, and berated my moms and me.

I, to this day, have never asked why he acted the way he did because I guess that I always hoped it would get better. I did not like the arguing and language used, and many nights I would punch holes in walls and doors simply because I could not punch him. I got whoopings until about age sixteen; then all of that had to stop. When I knew I was a little bigger and could handle myself, I vividly remember telling him one day as he attempted to hit me with a belt that if that belt so much as touched any part of my body, I would stand over his lifeless body and laugh. I knew that remark was grim, disturbing, and somewhat sociopathic.

For some strange reason, though, I could not help it. I had many homicidal fantasies about what would happen if I ever saw him hit moms or me again. I will spare you the details, but do know that I prayed to God on several occasions so that I would not engage in an irreversible act.

There was constant complaining about money. They involved arguments about who should pay what bill and why. In fact, these same arguments continue today. I know finances are a major topic of discussion in many homes, but it seemed to be the driving force behind every conversation, mostly negative conversations, in our home. That is why my motivation to be financially stable is so strong. I want to make it so that conversation never has to be negative. There was constant arguing over why he never came to any of my or my sister's sporting events. I would always wish that he would come to more games, but I justified it in my mind by telling myself that he had to figure out a way to provide for the family, and he did not really have extra time to watch us participate in athletic events. It was tough to live in such an environment.

I know I am not the only one who lived through such nonsense, and I recognize that there will be many after us who have to deal with the same things. To all of you who handled whatever negative home situations you were in, I applaud you for your efforts, strength, and personal convictions to make a difference. I know it was not easy, but you were made a better person because of it. To those of you who will undoubtedly endure such hardships, I say to you be strong and of good courage. Know that everything really does happen for a reason, and that which does not kill you, truly does make you stronger. Know that you have a purpose. Know that you create your own destiny and that your search for meaning will allow you to create and walk a path that can never be taken by another. Your journey, just as my journey, will be unique and will afford you the opportunity to write your name in history. Believe in yourself and know that time will take care of everything. Give time time, and I promise you that no matter how hard it is and/or how hard it gets, you will make it.

"To whom much is given, much is required." I was told that as an inspirational ploy by my basketball coach while I was a senior in high school. I felt that he used it to demean me; I used it as added fuel to the already sweltering fire. Why attempt to use a biblical reference in the wrong context—especially to a kid? I understand that statement, in and of itself, is absolutely true. In this particular instance, however, I was not given anything. I worked extremely hard to make myself a better human, a better student, and a better athlete. I couldn't fathom why he would say that I had been "given" anything. Oftentimes, the doctrine of unintended consequences can really lead to just that: unintended consequences. He thought that his words would make me panic and lose sight of my goals but, in reality, it did the exact opposite; it fanned a fire that will never go out. This is just one of the many instances where I learned to not take things personally, but let's start from grade nine.

Just the thought of entering high school made me apprehensive. Being at the bottom of the top and having to prove myself all over again was a welcomed challenge, but also potentially disastrous. Although I knew I had the potential to play three sports and dominate in all three, the idea of not knowing can sometimes be paralyzing to an individual. In elementary school, I did not consider myself an athlete and still do not to this day. I have always considered myself a gladiator. What is the difference, you ask? An athlete plays a game to have fun and, hopefully, win. Gladiators play to dominate. They attempt to render their opponent helpless, relying solely on mercy. There is no such thing as friendly competition. No one plays just for the sake of playing. If you are going to play, you might as well play to win. Even having that mentality, I was still nervous. If I only knew that athletics were going to be the least of my worries, I would have been better off.

As a freshman, I was enrolled in honors classes, new to the idea of hollering at girls, and also on the JV soccer team. Everything was moving smoothly until about one month into the school year. That is when life, from the eyes of a fourteen-year-old, almost ended. On 7 September 1994, I dropped my geometry class because I thought it was too hard. That's not the issue. The problems came into play when I told my mother what I did. Being who she is, even the idea of me not completing something that I started drove her absolutely insane. She called my counselor at school, told him to re-enroll me in the class, and let him know that under no circumstances was I ever allowed to drop any class. I was furious. At the time, math was not a strength of mine, and I had to spend exorbitant amounts of time studying just to be able to kind of understand what was going on. I felt like she and my counselor wanted me to fail. Unbeknownst to me, they knew I was capable of success and wanted to instill the idea of persistence and resilience in me at an early age. Whatever, though. I didn't care. I did not want to take the class and as a fourteen-year-old, future planning was not a major priority. My mother and I got into an intense argument about the class, and I told her to not worry about coming to the soccer game that evening. She reminded me that I should watch what I say and told me she was not coming to the game anyway.

I walked out of the house mad as hell, and my dad took me to the soccer game. Everything in the game was going fine until about ten minutes to go. I was playing well, and the team was playing well. Everyone was having a good time. I got the ball on the right side of the field, slid past the first defender, tricked the second defender, and got within scoring range. There was nothing to stop me—other than a mishap on my part or a spectacular play by the goalie. Well, there was no mishap, but the goalie did make a play—spectacular... I would say not. This is the vision you should see. I was 5'3" and maybe 105 lbs at the time. The goalie was about 6'2" and about 170 lbs. I planted my right foot, swung to kick with my left foot, but the follow-through never happened because the goalie slid into me; my right leg was tangled in between his legs, and my knee snapped. I and everyone else at the game knew that my knee was broken—in more than one spot. Pain is not even the appropriate word to describe the feeling. Excruciating, agonizing, unbearable to the point of tears is what I can say to make you understand. It was about 95 degrees outside, and I went into shock. Shaking, crying, confused, wondering why what happened just happened... to me. And the worst part of it all, my mom was not there to make it better. My dad even called her to come to the hospital, but she wouldn't. Although I know it was killing her on the inside, she was teaching.

- Lesson number one: Don't say things that you don't really mean.

- Lesson number two: Never disrespect your parents.

- Lesson number three: Never give up.

- Lesson number four: Believe in yourself always.

During my stay, I learned that I tore my ACL, broke two bones, and I was going to need surgery on 22 September 1994. Heartbreaking to a fourteen-year-old. I went home in a cast and stayed in it for nine months. The anger subsided, and Mom was again the best mom in the world; she even rubbed my feet for me at night until I fell asleep. Well, that stopped about five months in because one night she caught herself rubbing the wrong foot. I just laughed until I went to sleep.

The injury was a blessing in disguise. While stuck in a cast for so long, all I was able to do was focus on my schoolwork and learn how to handle adversity. Little did I know, that was only a sneak peek at adversity. There would be many more mountains I would have to climb before becoming one with myself and gaining a stronger sense of self. But I digress. Because I did not have to practice every day, becoming the best at school became my number-one priority. I wanted to get all A's and be considered smart. I already knew that once I started playing sports again, I would excel at that; but I wanted to do something out of the ordinary: be a black kid at a private school with a 4.0 GPA. So my quest for excellence began. Also, while immobilized for such a long period of time, I grew six inches—from 5'3" to 5'9." While I knew I would do well in sports, I also recognized that being so small in stature could be a potential problem in the future. Being 5'9" wasn't so bad.

It wasn't an easy task to earn and maintain a high GPA. My class schedule was difficult. I had a lot of friends who demanded time, and I was in pain for the majority of my freshman year. It was a fun journey, though. I earned the GPA that I wanted, I met lifetime friends, and I was also considered one of the go-to students in regard to academic inquiry. Now it was time for the hard part. I had set such high standards for myself and expectations of me were, according to some, impossible to attain. I looked at the expectations as a challenge and was determined to make impossible possible. I worked extremely hard in rehabilitation to enhance my knee and overall leg strength; and by the start of my tenth grade year, I was once again ready to rock and roll.

The year began, and I was a new person—taller, stronger, faster, smarter, and willing and ready to take on all challenges. Life was good. My class schedule was difficult but manageable and, more importantly, I was no longer at the bottom of the food chain; I had moved up a notch in the world. I chose not to play soccer that year and decided basketball, along with excellent academic progress, would be my top priorities. Tireless, relentless, focused, and determined were all words to describe my pursuit of excellence. This was the point in my life when I decided that even when winning is illogical, losing was still far from optional. I learned how to handle adversity, and I became desensitized to the negative ways of the world, began applying the laws of attraction, stopped taking things personal, and retained my ability to refrain from being cynical. I began to understand that dwelling on the past would be a detriment to my future. I would tell myself when I ran into a wall to either move it, go through it, or climb over it. If I was able to do something about a situation I was in, I did something about it. If I was unable to do something about it, I didn't worry about it. That became my daily way of thinking and has been a source of guidance for me ever since.

Why did I become that way? It was not one particular instance that changed my way of thinking, but a culmination of events that drastically altered my thought process. I was tired of being let down. I was tired of people telling me that I could not do something. I was tired of feeling inferior to others. I was tired of feeling like I had no control over life situations so, in an effort to make my life easier, I made it easier. I learned to disregard my surroundings and maintain my focus. I stopped worrying about things that I truly had no control over. I did not adopt a conspiracy theorist attitude, but remaining naïve was no longer a viable alternative. Learning how the world worked and learning quick was what I had to do to survive. It was Darwinian evolution, a Winston Churchillian way of perceiving the world that made everything in my world okay. Only the strong survive; I learned it at the age of fifteen and still live by it now.

As basketball season rolled around, I was elated. I knew I was going to be the starting point guard on the JV basketball team; and the only reason I knew that I wasn't going to be on the varsity team was because I was injured as a freshman and didn't have the opportunity to prove that I was talented enough to play at a very high level at such a young age. That being said, I was more than ready and willing to prove my worth on the junior varsity level. I was cordial to my future teammates, but tried my best to dominate them every practice. I wanted to be the go-to guy, and I wanted everyone to know it. I wanted my teammates to defer to me in a close game and have confidence in knowing that if I had the ball in my hands during crunch time, I would make the right decision. I was smaller than almost everyone on the team, so I knew that I was going to have to work extra hard and do something more than special to stand out and make a positive name for myself. I played with a chip on my shoulder—like I was starving, and the only way I would be able to get food was by taking it. I did not do these things in a negative or destructive way, however. I was helpful to teammates, and I also was extremely coachable. I asked questions, listened when advised to do certain things, and learned from my mistakes so that I could become the best player that I could be. Life was good. I was scoring points, making the team better, getting more and more recognition from my teammates and friends, and doing what I loved to do: play basketball. Then *bang*... another bout with adversity.

About midway through the season, Coach came down with a mysterious case of hater-itis. I was leading the team in scoring, assists, minutes played, and I was a team captain. Having a young black kid be the star amongst a bunch of white kids—what a novel concept. But, hey, it was only 1995, so what was I thinking? He told me although I was playing well and we were winning, he thought I should be more of a team player. I was confused because my teammates never said anything about it. I was leading the team in assists at the time, so I could not have been playing too selfishly. Coach did not do anything drastic, but the subtle tactical changes were painfully obvious and hurtful to me. While I continued to start, he would take me in and out of games in an effort to rattle, or maybe even break, my confidence. Once I would start heating up, he would take me out. If I got too excited, he would take me out. If we went on a major run, he would take me out. Take me out, put me in, take me out, put me in. This was how the remainder of the season went. He did it so I wouldn't outshine the kids he wanted to shine. For those of you who have experienced being taken in and out of games, you have felt and understand the psychological impact it can have on a person—particularly a kid. I never harbored any animosity or resentment towards my teammates, but it saddened me to feel that I wasn't being afforded the same opportunities as some of them. I didn't have delusions of grandeur then, and I still don't. I, at times, felt betrayed and helpless because I was doing everything I knew how to do to be what I was told he wanted me to be, and for reasons unknown to me, it still wasn't enough. The real ploy to shatter my confidence came at the end of the season when I did not get moved up to varsity to be a part of the tournament team. Three of my classmates, who I was just as good as at the time, had played on the varsity team all year. No big deal. Good for them. Perry was about 6'4," Ean was about 6'3," and Steve was about 6'5" as sophomores, so their height warranted their placement on the varsity team. I never disputed that all year, but to not be moved up for one game…wow…I was in a state of disbelief. How does the team captain not get moved up? I still don't know. This is when I knew my high school basketball career was not going to be that easy. However, not playing was not a choice.

The year went on. I earned a 3.9-plus GPA and was happy with that. I wanted to excel academically and athletically. Goal accomplished. Although there were some roadblocks put in front of me on the field of competition, I still managed to do better than most. If there were no mountains to climb, I would have outshined everyone by a landslide. Oh well, you live and you learn. Sometimes it is more fun to swim against the current because once you make it to the shore, you will know that you earned everything and that nothing was given to you.

The summer before my junior year, the current varsity coach was released. What a blessing for me. Now don't get me wrong; I have never and will never wish ill will upon anyone, but he blatantly told me that I would never, and I repeat never, play under his guidance. He told me that I was too little, that my game wasn't polished enough, and he didn't have time to wait and see if I was going to grow. Again...wow. What type of sane individual tells a sixteen-year-old kid that? The worst part about him telling me that was the fact that I actually believed him, even though I would play extremely well against his varsity team. Either way, me not making it to the varsity level never happened because the coach was given the opportunity to excel elsewhere before he had the opportunity to destroy my dreams.

That made me wonder, *Who would be a suitable replacement?* After about thirteen seconds of deliberation, it was decided that my JV coach would be his replacement. Again...wow. So the guy who purposely or inadvertently (depending on perspectives) tried to steal my shine as a sophomore was going to be afforded those same opportunities for two more years. *Lucky me*, I thought.

I was ready for the challenge. I knew I was going to have to play at a high level to earn minutes on the team because there were three senior guards in front of me. I thought, *No big deal.* If the journey was too easy, it wouldn't have been worth taking. The summer workouts began. Every day, six to eight hours per day, I practiced. I ran. I worked on my ball handling so that it was instinctual and reactionary as opposed to planned. I worked on my jump shot. I worked on my strength. I did not want to have any perceived weaknesses because I knew if I did, he would find them and exploit them. And by him, I mean the coach. I did not want to give him any reason to doubt me.

August rolled around, and I was ready to roll. My class schedule was cool, I was confident in my academic and intellectual abilities, and the girls were finally starting to pay attention to me. I loved that.

I was so focused on doing well on the field of competition that I somewhat neglected my studies. I lost focus and ended up getting a C in my trigonometry class. Flip out is not even the appropriate term to describe what my mom did. She called my counselor, she yelled at me, and she called my coach and told him that I was no longer allowed to play basketball. Pause for a second. Up until this point, I have painted a negative picture of Coach. I have, in a sense, vilified him and made it seem like he conspired with the world to ruin my life. That is not entirely true. He is a wonderful human being, a mentor to many, and a loving father. Looking back on it now, I just think he had outside pressures on him, and I was the easiest target. Back to the story.

The only reason that I knew my mom was outraged is because he told me. I came to practice one day, and he told me, in a fatherly whisper, that he needed to talk to me. He said, "I hate to inform you, but your mother called and said you are no longer allowed to play basketball until you improve your grades."

Now mind you, I still had a 3.7-plus GPA. All A's and one mishap. I could not believe it. One not so perfect grade, and no sports. I guess when you set the standard so high from the beginning, people begin to expect extraordinary and if you don't produce, problems arise. That is why my pursuit of excellence became relentless. I learned that not being number one, or as close to it as possible, was not acceptable in the Thomas household and in life in general, for that matter. I asked Coach and my counselor, who happens to be one of the best people to enter my life, to talk to my mom. I begged her to let me play, and they both assured her that I would never again falter academically. They were right. I never did.

Now basketball season was in full swing. I wasn't a starter, but I had worked hard enough to earn and maintain the sixth man position. I was cool with that. I was still smaller than everyone on the team, and sometimes player match-ups didn't allow me to play as much as I would have liked. I understood that and played my role. I was respected by my teammates as well as the competition. I was starting to get a hang of this basketball thing, but in my head, I knew that I needed a lot of work if I wanted to start, have a more than significant impact as a senior, and potentially play college basketball at the Division 1 level. I watched my teammates, listened to the coaching staff, asked questions, and worked vigorously to improve my game. I wanted to be the best, and nothing and/or no one was going to stop that. As I practiced and watched, I took a little bit of everyone's game and rolled it up into my own. I became a student of not only basketball, but of athletics in general. By watching other sports, I gained an in-depth understanding of what it meant to have exceptional footwork, eye-hand coordination, and the heart of a lion. I began to truly understand the importance of teamwork and how imperative relying on teammates had to be if we wanted to be a winning team. I slowly began to build my own ecosystem, a web of interdependency, in which we all knew that we had to depend and rely on each other if we ever wanted to actually win a high school championship. We had no such luck. We did not win the championship that year, but we went far in the tournament and had a strong foundation going into my senior year.

Complete transformation is how I would describe my level of confidence and game going into my senior year. While getting all A's in school remained a high priority, playing well enough during the season to be recognized and have the opportunity to play basketball at the Division 1 level became my only focus. School was easy. I knew I had the intellectual capacity to do well in that arena, so that was not a concern. I would focus, study, and get all A's. Anything less would have been uncivilized and, if you recall from a previous story, unacceptable. The summer began. My workouts remained intense, but this time, I added a separate element: a personal trainer.

Jason was cool as a fan. He was preparing to play professional football and knew what it was going to take for me to be a top-level athlete. He knew as well as I did what it was going to take for me to reach my potential, so he pushed me to the limit. I ran. I lifted. I shot hundreds of shots per day. I lifted some more. I became stronger, more athletic, more agile, faster, quicker, more confident, and an overall better player. My shine could not be denied...I thought. The overall enhancement to my skill level was quite noticeable. I was playing extremely well in summer league games and was floating on cloud forty-nine.

In an effort to really test my skills and validate my thoughts that I was really getting good at the game I loved, I decided I to go to a recruiting camp. Many top-level high school players were there, and the competition was extremely intense. Although I wasn't as highly touted as many of the other players, I knew that I was just as good if not better than most of them. All I needed and wanted was a chance to prove my worth. That opportunity came, and I took complete advantage of the situation. I shined in individual drills as well as team drills. Several coaches at the camp complimented me on a variety of my skills and abilities ranging from ball-handling to defense to shooting. Playing defense, handing the ball, and scoring were definitely strong suits of mine, and I knew if I had the chance to show it, someone would take notice. Just as I envisioned it, coaches took notice. I played very well during that camp and was rated as one of the top players. I made the all-star team and played as a starter. The best part about it was that my team won. This is how I first started to get noticed as a potential Division 1 basketball player. Before, it was just the dream of a kid. Now it was within my grasp, and I was determined to not let it slip away.

My first interaction with a couple of coaches from Notre Dame, which I kept completely to myself, took place at that camp. I was ecstatic and nervous all at the same time. Here I was, seventeen years old, alone in a city to which I had never been, and trying to sell myself to coaches from a top level Division 1 program. I remember after the all-star game one of the coaches wearing an "ND" monogrammed shirt came up to me and said, "Good game." I thanked him and asked him what my chances were of playing at such a high level, particularly Notre Dame. He told me that my chances were decent and advised that I work on my strength. I couldn't even bench press 100 lbs at the time and only weighed about 135 lbs... maybe. He also told me that Notre Dame's roster was full of scholarship athletes and if I was fortunate enough to make the team, it would be as an "invitational walk-on." While I knew I could play at many other schools, playing at ND would afford me the opportunity to have the best of both worlds: gain an education from a top scholastic university and play in the Big East. The thought alone made me smile and gave me even more reason to want to work hard to make it happen. Plus, I didn't have anything to lose. No one other than me, Ray (the AAU coach and personal trainer at Berston Field House), and my parents believed that I could do it. The crazy thing about my transformation was it all came from a kid who said I was not going to be able to do something. Talk about motivation. Talk about adding fuel to the fire. I did not even want to eat regular food because I felt it would be more productive if I just fed off the hate. One day while we were in open gym during the summer, we were shooting around and, as usual, people were joking around and talking. All of the jokes came to a screeching halt when Casey told me, with a straight face, that he didn't think I would be good enough to play ball in college. Again... wow. My quest for excellence and an even deeper desire to succeed came because of the words of one boy, a teammate, a "friend." I am sure that you have heard the euphemism "Sticks and stones may break my bones, but words will never hurt me." That statement could not be further from the truth. I was devastated, hurt, and confused as to why my "friend," someone who I had passed the ball to for several wide-open three pointers, would say something like that. He told me a few years later that he was joking, but the day he said it, he was more than sincere. To say that it tore me up on the inside would be an understatement. He might as well have ripped my heart out, chewed it up, swallowed it, threw it up, chewed it up again, and finally digested it.

To the outside world, nothing was wrong. During high school, I knew that I was the topic of discussion for many families other than my own, so I was used to it. I knew I was the cause of envy for some students and, as a result, when certain things were said about me, it did not offend me. People saw me walk around like nothing was bothering me, and I loved it that way. I enjoyed people seeing me as mysterious because my personal life was unknown. They were intrigued, I think. I heard Casey's words and replayed them repeatedly in my mind while I trained with Jason. During summer league games or outside in my backyard, I would say those words to myself: "Not good enough, not good enough." On the inside of books that I read, I wrote the words, "Not good enough, huh? ... Time will tell." I was determined to prove another individual wrong. As the summer wore on, I continued to play ball at a high level and prepare myself for my senior season. When it came, I was ecstatic.

In November 1997, my senior year officially began. I was known in the city, my grades were good, my girlfriend was good, my game was nice, and I was ready to make it happen. We started the season out on a tear. We were undefeated through, I think, our first ten conference games of the season, and things were going great. Four out of our five starters were averaging double digits, and a couple of my teammates were averaging double-doubles—very impressive. We were getting it. Then we lost. No big deal. We didn't panic. We continued to play our game the way we knew how and then *bang*, a photographer accidentally put me on the front cover of the sports page in the newspaper a few games in row. There wasn't a public outcry for my crucifixion, but there d*** sure had to be a private one. After the third photograph, Coach "try to steal a kid's dream," as I sometimes called him in my younger years, called me into his office. This is when he told me, "For of those to whom much is given, much is required." I was perplexed, bewildered, confused, puzzled, and mystified because, as previously mentioned, I knew that I had not been *given* anything. I earned my starting spot. I worked hard to become one of the best players on the team. I earned all A's in school. The only thing that has ever been given to me is the title "God's child." Coach went on to tell me that he wanted me to "run the show and not be the show."

Again... wow. If the current methods are working and producing wins, why question those methods? I still have not figured out that answer. He told me that he felt I was becoming conceited and was no longer working as hard as I should have been working. Check this out, though. I was always the first one at practice, the most vocal, the most coachable, and the last to leave. I worked with my teammates to help them become better players, and no one worked harder on their game than I did. I am not saying that my other teammates did not work extremely hard to improve themselves as well, because they did. All I am saying is that I was not, in any way, slacking in my workout habits.

I was also voted in as team captain. Last time I checked, in a democracy, an individual cannot put himself in a position of leadership, power, and/or privilege unless the public agrees. Therefore, in my biased opinion, his sentiments were without merit. They were simply another gesture to derail my self-confidence. Next game, we lost. That was the ammunition he needed. He told me a few days later that he was going to make some changes to the starting lineup, and I was going to come off the bench. Again... wow. I was mad and sad at the same time. My confidence did not falter, and I did not second-guess myself. His judgment and decision-making abilities, however, were in serious question. The next few games, I was given the opportunity to play as the sixth man. Coach was trying to prove a point. His intentions, from my vantage point, were to prove to me that we could win without my services. I knew that was incorrect. I may not have been the best player on the team, but I was valuable and valued (at least I like to think so). To his utter amazement, we lost more of those games than we won. Now, because we were losing, he had to do something quick to maintain his reputation and get us back on the winning track. I went back into his office, and he told me that he was going to re-insert me into the starting lineup. Duh. I could have told him that. Pause for reflection. – As I think back on that time in my life, Coach taught me a valuable lesson: – never stop trying to be qualified for your job. Maybe as a young boy, I thought that I was working hard, but he knew I was capable of more. It is, often times, difficult to be objective when you are the one in the situation, particularly when emotions have taken over. As I grow wiser, I understand that there is always a lesson to be learned. We just have to pay attention and listen. "To whom much is given, much is required." I understand now. Back to the story. Oh my, how quickly the tables turned, because now I knew I had the upper hand. He knew that he could not win without me, and I knew that I was needed. Did I take advantage of that situation, you wonder? I surely did. I did not react negatively to my teammates, but I had lost all respect for the coaching staff and athletics administration. I became more vocal in practice, did what I wanted to do within reason, and blocked him out every time he attempted to talk to me. All I heard in huddles was, "Blah blah blah on three … defense."

I played my game, and we returned to winning games. I ran the show and tried to be the show. He might not have liked it, but he surely had to live with it. Unluckily, one of our better players broke his jaw near the end of the season, and we also needed him to win. Without his nightly double-double, we were, in a sense, crippled. We made it to regionals, but were unable to pull off the victory. Season was over. Unfortunately, we were unable to make it to the mountaintop, but we gave it our best shot. There is never a need to walk around with your head down when you do all you can to be the best you can. I was proud of what we had accomplished as a team and was ready to prepare for the next challenge—further enhancing my game in an effort to play basketball at the Division 1 level.

After school was over my senior year and my acceptance into Notre Dame was official, Ray began pushing me and working on my behalf more than anyone I had met in my life up to that point, other than family members. I worked out about six hours per day, and he was constantly on the phone talking to coaches about me. His efforts allowed me to speak to several different Division 1 coaches. The hard work was finally starting to pay dividends. He would have coaches come to watch me work out, and he would invite them to summer league games. I went from a docile kid to a wolf. I knew I could play basketball, and there was not anyone or anything that was going to stop me from doing it.

We all need someone in our lives who believes in us more than we believe in ourselves, and Ray was that person for me. He was loyal, brutally honest, helpful, a teacher, a mentor, and a friend. He groomed me and turned me into a fighter. He is another person to whom I am forever grateful. I weighed my options and told Ray that I wanted to be a Fighting Irishman. He asked why several times and reiterated to me that if I went there as opposed to some of the other schools, I would have to pay at least for my first year. I told him I understood all of that, but I knew it was going to be the best place for me. I do not know how I knew or what made me even think that, but my intuition was talking to me, and I had to listen and act accordingly. He no longer questioned my intentions and began to work on getting me on the team at ND. At one point, without my knowing, he wrote a letter on my behalf, sent footage of me playing, and told the coaches I was 6'2" and 180 lbs. That might not sound like a big deal, but at that time, I was 5'9"/5'10" and about 135 lbs. His intentions were good, though, and he wanted the best for me, even if it meant boosting numbers a tiny bit. Even the coaches thought that was funny when I went into the office the first week of school. They showed me the letter and the footage of my workouts and game tapes. They were more than impressed that I had someone who believed in me that much that he would go through so much trouble to get my name out there and make my dreams become a reality.

It was almost time to begin the next chapter in my life, and I knew what I had to do. I worked out tirelessly. I lifted, I ran, I shot jump shots, I worked on my ball handling skills, I barely slept. I felt like a prisoner in my own mind. When my body wanted to quit, the words *"you aren't good enough"* screamed at me, and quitting became an afterthought. I had the desire, will, and determination to succeed against all odds. In my mind, there was no other option. I thought about it every day. I dreamed about it every night. My motivation to do what was supposedly unable to be done and a desire to channel negative energy into something positive were the driving forces behind my hunger. I saw success in my mind, so I knew that it was only a matter of time before my inner thoughts manifested themselves in my outward reality. I was headed to the University of Notre Dame.

VISUALIZE AND IT WILL MATERIALIZE

College began and once again, I felt alone. I didn't know what to think, I didn't know what to expect, and I definitely was unsure of how living away from home was going to work. My class schedule looked next to impossible, and did I mention that I didn't know a soul on the Notre Dame campus? The only people that I had even talked to were the basketball coaches. They knew my desire to play at the Division 1 level; and although the roster was full and there were not any more scholarships available, they told me that I had the talent to play and that I would have to prove myself. I will get back to that story in a little while.

Anyway, school began. I moved into Morrissey Manor and met my two roommates, Pat and Mark. We got along great. There was only one problem: we all had our beds and dressers in one room. Initially, we thought this was a genius idea and figured we would use the other room for common space—an area where we could chill, hang out with girls, and just relax. That situation worked for about two weeks. It sucked. It especially sucked for me because I was in the middle bunk. Without fail, about four times a week I would wake up to go and use the bathroom and almost rip my head off by hitting it on the bottom of the top bunk. Either way, something had to be done immediately, if not sooner.

I cannot remember if we played rock, paper, scissors, drew straws, flipped a coin, or had a mental challenge to see who could say their ABC's backward the fastest in order to get the other room and do away with the common space. Maybe I won the challenge, or maybe it was because I was the only black dude in our section, and they didn't want any problems. All I know is that I won, and I was ecstatic. I proceeded to move my bed into the other room and set it up. I even had it set up so that my bed was like nine feet in the air, and my closet space and computer space were under me. Seems like a bright idea, right? Well it was eventually, but initially it was terrible. Being three feet from the ground to nine feet in the air took some getting used to. The first week, I fell out of that bed and hit the floor hard not once, not twice, but four times. My phone would ring, and I would think that I could just quickly grab it like I used to when I was in the middle bunk but, unfortunately, all I felt was air until I hit the ground, the sink, or a combination of the two. Pat and Mark came to the rescue the first two times, but they just laughed after fall numbers three and four. I couldn't blame them. It was kind of funny. After fall number four, I bought an extension cord and had my phone right up on the bed with me. I also put a protective railing next to the bed so that I wouldn't accidentally hit the ground again. So, yes... I finally figured out how to stay safe while sleeping.

Once I figured out the whole sleeping situation, I began to meet people in my dorm: Andy, JC, crazy Dave, ROTC Dave, Wes, Kurt, and Josh. These were the guys who made college life easy and fun for me throughout my entire freshman year. I am sure they don't know it, but they kept me happy, comfortable, and gave me that feeling of family that I so desperately needed that year. I was sad, I wasn't eating right, school was much more difficult than I anticipated, I was lonely even in the midst of a crowd, and I felt that I didn't really deserve to be there. If it weren't for those guys and some of the guys on the basketball team, I would have quit and went back home. Lucky for me, God saw fit to bless me and put me around a group of people that were motivated and wanted to succeed in this world as well. So, fellas, if you are reading this, I want to say thank you a million times. Even though I have not seen many of you since college, I want you to know that I appreciate you and will forever value all of you as friends. Now, since that sentimental moment is over, let's get back to the story.

FRESHMAN YEAR

As I tried to ingratiate myself to the coaches and solidify a spot on the basketball team, they told me what I already knew. They told me that the roster was full of scholarship players and, if I proved myself to them, I would be invited to be a member of the team. I was advised that due to NCAA rules and regulations, I would not be allowed to actually lift weights with the team, but I would be able to scrimmage with them every day. They told me to lift weights, run, and get on the same regimen they were doing, only I would have to do it individually for a while. I was perfectly fine with that. I was used to working out alone, anyway. The first day I went to the gym to play with the team, I was starstruck. I was actually in a gym full of Division 1 basketball players, and I was going to actually play with them. Well, that is what I thought, anyway. I thought that since one of the coaches introduced me to everyone, my road to making the team was going to be easy. Completely wrong is an understatement.

That first day I sat there for three hours, watched them play, and didn't run up and down the court one time. *Oh well, there is always tomorrow*, I thought. I went back to the gym the next day, but this time I got there early. I got on the court and started shooting like I belonged. I think this caught the attention of some of the upperclassmen because they actually came up to me and started talking to me. They told me that they liked my attitude, thought that I had a nice shot and all of that, and they would *try* to get me on the court today. I smiled and was like, "Cool." I didn't want to seem too desperate. I knew I was good enough to play, and I just waited patiently. Day two: no action. *Oh well, there is always tomorrow,* I thought.

Day three came along and, again, I was there early shooting and working on ball-handling drills. The guys came in, picked teams, and began to play. I watched and bingo, one of the guards went down with a twisted ankle. I was the only other point guard in the gym at the time, so I had to play. Preparation finally met opportunity, and I was ready to get it done. There was no fear, only a dream that was now absolutely real. I looked on the floor of the Joyce Center to see the ND insignia and had a Notre Dame Division 1 point guard guarding me, and I felt as if I was one of them. I knew I belonged. A kid from Flint, who many believed could not play at such a high level, was about to prove everyone wrong and make that team. There was no doubt in my mind.

From that moment on, I won the heart of everyone on the team except one person—the starting point guard. I, to this day, do not know why he didn't take a liking to me at first. He couldn't have been threatened by me. I was not even technically on the team yet; he was bigger than me, stronger than me and, above all, the starting point guard for ND. Either way, I played extremely hard against him and was just as offensively skilled as he was. I made him work for baskets, and I made him work to guard me. I was very elusive and quick when I started college, so I know it was difficult for him to guard me. I would call home and tell moms, "I don't know why he doesn't like me." She would say just keep playing hard, be respectful, and he will come around sooner or later.

This went on for a couple of weeks, and finally I knew what would make him join my team. I sat down with him and asked him how I could become a Notre Dame point guard. I sincerely asked him questions and tried to get him to understand that I just wanted to be welcomed and part of something special—a group of guys all ready and willing to accomplish the same goal. He told me how difficult it was to play at such a high level, how hard classroom work was, how difficult weight training was, and how much fun it could all be. We didn't become friends immediately after that conversation, but the wall had fallen down, and I knew everything was going to be all right. He began to do shooting drills with me and talked to me about college life. I had made another friend—someone I knew that I would be able to trust in the future.

I continued to practice with the team every day. Only now, they were actually picking me to play, and I was no longer merely a spectator. I felt like I was one of them, and they accepted me into their group. I loved it and cherished every moment of it. "For Notre Dame, at guard, number five from Flint, Michigan, Charles Thomas"—I liked saying that to myself, and I said it over and over again. Even before I knew what the law of attraction was, I practiced it. I knew that positive thoughts would bring positive things into my life, and I was ready for everything ND had to offer—good, bad, or indifferent. Opportunities such as the one I was presented with do not come that often, so when they do, you have to be ready to seize the moment. You have to freeze it and own it and for however long it is, you have to consider that minute golden.

As I mentioned, I continued to practice with the team every day. After we would leave the gym, I would eat, do some homework, go lift weights, and practice some more. I would work on everything as if I was learning to play the game for the first time. This routine became set in stone for me and remained that way from August until October when it was time to go home for fall break. I did not want to leave campus because I assumed that I would not be able to practice as much at home because of family time and outside influences. Either way, I told myself that I had worked as hard as I could and proven myself to the guys. Hopefully when tryouts came around the week after fall break, I would shine and be offered a spot on the team. The rest was left up to God, and I knew He would come through for me, so there were no worries on my end.

Three days into fall break, my mom and I were in the kitchen getting ready for a high school basketball game. I remember it like it was yesterday. Moms was sitting in the chair putting her shoes on, and I was standing up looking out the window. I was wearing some Gary Payton shoes, blue Adidas warm-up pants, and a yellow Notre Dame zip-up sweatshirt. It was such an exciting and defining moment in my life, how could I possibly have forgotten even the smallest detail? It's impossible. I can never forget.

Like I said, I was standing in the kitchen talking to Moms when the phone rings. The voice on the other end said, "May I speak to Charles?"

I'm like, "Yeah, this is me. Who is this?"

He said, "BT."

Now, I have a friend named BT, but he was young like me at the time and this was a grown man on the phone, so I said, "Come on, man, stop playing, fa' real... Who is this? I don't have time to be playing on the phone because me and Moms about to go to a game."

He was like, "It's Coach BT from Notre Dame."

I was speechless. All I could do was apologize and tell him I thought somebody was trying to play like they were my friend, BT. He laughed it off and proceeded to tell me that an actual walk-on tryout was unnecessary for me. He explained that I had proven myself enough through playing in pick-up games and working out.

He said, "The guys love you, the coaching staff loves you, and we think you would be an asset to the program."

I was still speechless, and that doesn't happen often—hardly ever, actually. He told me to come back to school the following day and be ready for practice. "What number do you want, by the way?" he asked.

"Number five," I replied. For Notre Dame, at guard, number five from Flint, Michigan, Charles Thomas. A dream was slowly but surely turning into a reality. No matter what happened from this point forward, I knew that giving in to any type of pressure was not an option. I am sure some people wanted me to fail, and I am sure others wanted me to succeed. The only thing that I knew with absolute certainty was that I was a student-athlete at the University of Notre Dame, and nothing was going to stop me from succeeding in life and living life to the fullest. A kid from Flint, Michigan, had not only been accepted to one of the most prestigious universities in the U.S., but he was also a member of the men's varsity basketball team. From nothing to something, dreams do come true; without that possibility, nature would not incite us to have them (John Updike). All you have to do is ask, work hard, pray, and know that it will come true. Do that, and I promise you the universe will conspire to help you.

The next day, I was back on campus. As I write this, the same emotions that I experienced in October of 1998 come rushing back to me: elation, excitement, joy, apprehension, uncertainty, and a feeling of "I told you so." The tables had turned. People were no longer saying, "You can't do that," or "There is no way in hell to accomplish that." Instead their words transformed into, "How in the hell did you do that?" I will tell you how in four words, which I have tattooed on my chest: faith, desire, resilience, patience. Many people would have folded and given up if facing the odds I faced, but I had nothing to lose. I had too many people who cared about me and I knew what I wanted, so not getting it wasn't an alternative for me. In my mind, it was never a long shot; my goals then and now are always well within my reach. I just have to make sure I hold on to them once I grab them.

I got back to campus and other than some of the athletic teams, only a few students were still on campus during fall break. I unpacked my bags and got to the gym to join the team for practice. I walked in, and the experience was surreal; the team clapped, some of the guys hugged me like a younger brother, and everyone welcomed me with open arms. I was in heaven. I, to this day, still feel as if I cannot accurately describe how I felt that afternoon, even though I oftentimes try. I cannot think of any other day in my life that was better other than the day I was born, and I don't actually remember that day—only heard about it. Although a lot of kids my age were playing basketball at a major Division I university, they were supposed to be there. I wasn't. I was given a list of reasons by adults and many of my peers as to why I would not make it. Had I listened to all of the haters, I wouldn't have made it. I was there, though, and loving every minute of it. Little did I know that the same joy I experienced would be the major cause of many of my pains.

My freshman year on the Notre Dame men's varsity basketball team wasn't what I thought it was going to be. Don't get me wrong; I wouldn't trade it for the world. I just always envisioned it differently in my head. I knew I wouldn't play much, but d***. I didn't think I was only going to play in one game. I didn't complain, though. I was the youngest, and by far the smallest, on the team. I had the most to learn and was ready and willing to do just that. I didn't travel with the team that year, but I practiced and worked on my game every day. Some days, Coach would call and say I didn't need to come to practice that day; but even on those days, I would go to the Rock and work tirelessly to make myself a better player. I did not want to have any pronounced weaknesses to my game. If there were to be any criticisms, I wanted it to be on the fact that I wasn't 6'5," and I couldn't have cared less about that because I couldn't do anything about it. That was all God's doing, and since I knew that, I just worked with the package that He gave me and tried to make the best of it.

On my days off, after class, I would lift with T-Ro, our strength and conditioning coach; I would run; I would do any and everything possible to increase my chances of playing. I would talk to the older guys on the team and emulate their individual workouts.

My goal was to make a significant contribution to the program as a sophomore. The coaches recognized and constantly complimented me on my improvements as a basketball player; the guys told me I was doing a good job, and T-Ro made sure I was getting stronger so that I would not get pushed around as much.

My first year was rocky because it was a first-time experience. I was doing okay academically, but I was homesick and knew I could have been doing better. My parents were struggling financially to keep me in school, and that was eating me up inside because although I was trying my best to make a better situation for myself, my best, at that time, wasn't good enough. Here I was, going to one of the most expensive universities in the country, playing with top-level basketball players every day, and my parents were struggling to keep me in school. I knew it and at one point told Coach that I was going to have to leave the university because my parents could not afford paying such high tuition costs.

Unbeknownst to me, Mom sold her Cadillac, and my parents took some of the equity out of the house to keep me in school. At that moment, I truly knew the love that parents have for their children. No matter how tenuous a relationship may have been in the past, good parents will go to hell and back to ensure that their children have every opportunity to succeed. You would think that I would have been grateful to them too, huh? Not so much. I was irate, actually. "Why would you sell your car and take equity out of the house when I could have just left and went to a cheaper university?" was the question I asked of my parents.

"Because we felt like it, and last time I checked, you don't pay any bills around here" was the response I was given.

Case closed. I didn't have a response to that. I just told myself that I had to do whatever necessary to make sure that all of the people who sacrificed to make life easier for me were not disappointed and were taken care of in the future. On the court, we weren't doing so well, either. We were doing better than previous years, but not as well as we should have done. We were 14-16 that year and did not get invited to the NIT tournament or the NCAA tournament. When the season was drawing to a close, I had a sit-down conversation with Coach. He told me that he was really impressed with how I had progressed throughout the season, and he was looking forward to me making a significant contribution as a sophomore—music to my ears. That was exactly what I wanted to hear. He told me that I would have the opportunity to be put on a full athletic scholarship and no longer have to worry about financial issues. Again, exactly what I wanted to ear. Was he misleading me? I don't think so, but I will never know because about one month after that talk, he resigned. That was not what I wanted to hear. I knew I had another mountain to climb.

Was I ready? Yes. Did I want to? No, I absolutely did not. Did I do it? Yes, because I didn't have a choice.

SOPHOMORE YEAR

I walked into my sophomore year of college not knowing what to expect. Was I going to be only a full-time student, or would I once again have the opportunity to be a full-time student athlete? I wasn't 100 percent certain. I knew I would do well academically because that has never been a concern of mine. I am not saying that I didn't think that my class schedule wasn't going to be difficult, because I knew it was. I am merely saying that I was disciplined and focused enough to efficiently and effectively handle my academic workload. The apprehension came into play when I thought about the field of competition also known as the basketball court.

A few weeks went by, and there was no word as to who might be the new Notre Dame men's basketball coach. There was speculation, but nothing concrete. I didn't really care. I just wanted the chance to talk to the new coach to get a better understanding of where he was mentally. Prior to Coach leaving, I was told horror stories about one coach leaving and a new coach replacing all of the current players on the team, especially those who hadn't made a significant contribution the prior year. Those stories were always in the back of my mind, so I stepped up the intensity of my workouts. When the new coach saw me play and inquired about my academic background, I wanted him to tell his staff that I was definitely a keeper. So again, I went to class, studied hard, worked out harder than ever, and knew that I would make it. After a few weeks of speculation, it was announced that Kansas assistant, Coach D, was going to be our new head coach. At the time, everyone was excited because he was given raving reviews in virtually every collegiate sporting magazine. He vowed to put Notre Dame basketball back on the map and commented that his would be the best-conditioned team in the Big East conference. He even called some of the players' parents individually to formally introduce himself. When my mother met him, she was immediately enchanted by his charm and charisma. My dad—not so much. He told me early on there was something different about this guy, but he just couldn't put his finger on it. His feelings were correct, and every member on the team found out what that something different was by the end of the season.

Within his first couple of weeks on the job, Coach D talked to each player individually. When it was my turn, I could not wait to talk to him and see what he had to say about his vision for the program and, more importantly, me as a player. I sat down in his office, and he began to tell me how he wanted to the program to be considered an elite program not only in the Big East, but also nationally. He explained how coaching and teaching were his passion, and he would not settle for anything less than 100 percent effort by anyone on his team. He told me that he talked to the previous coaching staff about me, and he also told me that he talked to my professors about my academic standing. He was impressed with what he was told and knew that I would work hard. He was extremely charming, charismatic, and confident.

He spoke very matter-of-factly and seemed to be on top of his game. He proceeded to tell me that no one had a guaranteed spot on the team, not even the starters from the previous year. He explained that practice time would be the tryout for everyone. Before the conversation, I already assumed he would say that, so it did not come as a surprise. Plus, nothing in my life had come easy, so why would I have expected this situation to be any different? I asked him if I would have the opportunity to earn an academic scholarship like I had talked about with the previous coaching staff. He told me yes, but I would have to prove myself to him first. Cool, easy, not a problem. I knew I was going to have to do that, anyway. He was a master psychologist. He said all of the right things at precisely the right time and looked you directly in the eye when he said it. I told my parents everything that was said during the conversation, but my dad still was not convinced. Maybe because he was also a charmer, he had some sort of special radar that could readily detect deceit in an individual. He simply told me to be careful and to not believe everything I was told by the coach because it might not necessarily be true. My dad was correct.

After about two weeks of practice, he let us know who was going to be on the team and, as I had planned, I was a part of it. As I have already mentioned, everyone was ecstatic to have a new coach who was well-respected in the industry and knew the game of basketball. We knew that he would push us to our maximum potential, but we never anticipated a Dr. Jekyll and Mr. Hyde-type personality. Off the court, for the most part, he was a complete gentleman and fatherly figure. On the court, however, he was a tyrant, a power-hungry egomaniac. I attribute his many lapses in judgment to the fact that this was his first major Division 1 head coaching position, and he wanted so desperately to do well that he forgot he was coaching kids with feelings and not robots. I am sure I speak for many of my teammates when I say he made our lives absolute hell for an entire season. There were days when he would make me feel like I shouldn't have ever been born.

In an effort to be funny and probably as motivation to the other guards on the team, he would say things like "Are you f***** serious? Are you really going to let him score on you like that? He is a 'walk-on' for Christ sake." Or he would say, "You gotta be f***** kidding me. You are going to let him score on you like that? You ought to be ashamed of yourself."

I know what he was trying to do, but I don't think he fully understood the impact his words had on me as a person. He did not realize that what he was saying could have lowered my self-esteem tremendously. Maybe he didn't care. Lucky for me, I was a strong-willed person. Some of my teammates, on the other hand, weren't as mentally tough as I was and to this day still harbor feelings of hatred in their heart toward him. Like I said, he didn't just do this to me, so maybe I shouldn't have felt so bad, but I did. Not only was I not playing the minutes that I knew I deserved, but his level of respect for me and others on the team was somewhere between negative one million and infinite. He would even insult our star player as a form of motivation—wrong method, Coach. That type of motivation bred resentment and forced a couple of cats to transfer, and it almost led several others to quit.

The worst of the days came after a loss to an exhibition team known as Marathon Oil. The point guard on that team scored forty points and, by the way, did I mention that we lost? I sure wish we wouldn't have lost that day. We were supposed to have the next day off, but we didn't. We were told to be at the gym at 6:00 a.m. and as we were instructed, we all were there bright and early. There should have been a sign on the locker room door saying: "Beware, psycho personality day." At least we would have all been warned, but there was no such sign and/or warning. We were completely blindsided.

After stretching, he told us to get on the line and that we were going to run until he was tired of blowing the whistle. The resounding response was filled with angry cuss words. This was the day I was no longer considered a "walk-on" by anyone closely associated with the Notre Dame men's varsity basketball program. There were a total of five "walk-ons" on the team that year, including myself. None of us played in the loss to Marathon Oil, and none of the other "walk-ons" had to run. Guess what? I did. This was the day I officially earned my stripes. I had to go to war with the fellas, and we all came out alive. For two hours, we ran. Sprint after sprint after sprint. Guys were throwing up purple stuff, people were falling down from exhaustion, and the entire time he thought it was funny. Again, wrong motivational method, Coach. What he didn't realize was that it pulled us together as a team, and now he became the enemy.

At one point during the marathon, one of my teammates asked if we could take a break to get some water. Coach said, "Take a break for some water? F*** no, but I sure would like to have a sip."

He had one of the managers bring him a cup of water and while we were running, he would take loud gulps and say, "Ahhhh." I am not demonizing the man, I am merely telling a story to illustrate a point; at that particular juncture in his life and coaching career, he was an unstable creature.

Three hundred and four sprints later, we were done. Physically and emotionally, we were all drained. Here is the worst part about it. After we were all laying there, he began to cry and tell us that instead of taking his son to the Disney on Ice production, he was at the gym with a bunch of a******s.

Again, wrong motivational tactic, Coach. I hate to be the bearer of bad news, but after running three hundred and four sprints, not one player in that gym cared about him, his family, his religious beliefs and/or affiliations, or his favorite Disney production.

We just wanted to go home and sleep—if we could conjure up the spirits to help us walk back. I remember it like it was yesterday. It is funny to look back on it and laugh now, but on that day, it may have been many things, but funny was not one of them.

I dealt with the barrage of insults, negative remarks, condescending comments, and tyrannical guidance that year. I was told to take my earrings out, cut my hair, and not have so much fun, among other things. I continued to work hard, though. I never publicly showed any signs of weakness, but I was dying on the inside. I would go to the gym late at night after studying to simply work on my game and validate to myself that I was a good Division 1 basketball player. I am a realist. I knew that I was not a superstar, but I did know that I was good enough to play and make significant contributions. I would pray every night and ask God to take this burden away from me. I would constantly repeat in my mind during many practice sessions the old adage of "this too shall pass." I would not show any signs of weakness because he would have sniffed it out like a shark sniffing blood in the water.

Get this, though. One day he called me into his office, sat me down, and told me that he was going to put me on an athletic scholarship. "Say word," I responded, which meant I was in shock at the good news.

Apparently, he went to urban lingo class that day because he jokingly replied, "Word up."

Coach D was the first coach to put me on an athletic scholarship. For that, I will be forever grateful to him and he knows it, but he also knows I dealt with a lot of nonsense and potentially character defeating hardships. It was all for the good, though, because everything I dealt with that year made me a stronger and better human being. For that, I am thankful. Not too long after a 22-11 season and a trip to the NIT finals in Madison Square Garden in New York City versus Wake Forest, Coach D resigned his post as the Notre Dame head coach to take the head coaching job at his alma mater, the University of North Carolina. His stint there only lasted a few years because of what I believed to be personality and power issues. He was removed from coaching the upper echelon programs for a couple of years, but he has now found his way back into the upper ranks of collegiate basketball coaching. Congratulations, Coach. We all have to learn some kind of way. You taught me, life taught you, but we both learned.

JUNIOR YEAR

After his resignation, I am sure many people were excited, and rightfully so, but I thought, *Not again*. I was going to have to prove myself all over again to a new coach, who I was sure was going to come in and clean house. Here we go, another mountain to climb. Was I ready? Yes, I was ready. Did I want to? Absolutely not. Did I? I did not have a choice. The change all happened during the summer before my junior year. Coach D left, and we were once again playing the waiting game. We were all waiting to find out who the new coach was going to be. I strapped in, laced up, and was ready for another roller coaster ride. I was very optimistic, though. Remember Ray, my AAU coach who guided me and pushed me to levels of exhaustion that I never thought I was capable of reaching? Well, he wasn't so convinced that it was going to be my year to shine, so he put in calls to a few more major Division 1 universities and requested that they come to a few of my summer league games to watch me play. He even had a couple of coaches fly in to watch me practice and go through some of his individual workouts.

Despite what transpired during the previous two years, my level of confidence was soaring. I was an eagle flying alone and loving every second of it. I was playing well, and I knew it. Each coach that came to an individual workout or an actual summer league game was so impressed that they were actually willing to give me a full ride athletic scholarship to attend their university. I declined because at that point, I was already a Fighting Irishman. I wanted to earn a Notre Dame degree, and I wanted to be more than just an athlete at some university. I wanted to make a difference and a positive name for myself as a University of Notre Dame student-athlete. There was no disrespect to the other universities because they were all reputable programs. I would have also had the opportunity to step in, play, and make a significant contribution right away. I prayed about the situation and decided to stay. To me, leaving would have been a sign of weakness. I felt that if I would have left, I would have been running from a situation. In my mind, I had already done too much to turn back, and I had to try my best to optimize my situation. It wasn't going to be easy, but I didn't care.

After a few weeks of speculation, my third coach in three years was named. From day one, I knew Coach B was going to be cool. I was not sure how much I was going to play, if at all, but I knew he was a good person. There was no indication of a split personality, and he was one of the "what you see is what you get" type of cats. He was a straight shooter and never claimed to be anything else. Within his first week on the job, he called me to formally introduce himself as the new head coach. He told that he didn't consider me a "walk-on," and I was just as much a part of the team as anyone else. I asked him what my chances were of playing, and he said equal to every other guard on the team. I was a little skeptical because I had heard that story too many times before.

I prodded and questioned until he finally said, "Wow, the stories about you being persistent, determined, and motivated were real, huh?"

I could only laugh and respond, "Yes, sir."

After the conversation, I was more than comfortable in my decision to stay and remain a part of the Fighting Irish program. So again, I worked on my game until the point of exhaustion six days per week. I ran, I lifted, I worked on my ball-handling skills, I worked on my shooting, and I worked on my one-on-one moves. I was getting to be pretty good at the game that I loved so much. I was killing in summer league games and was respected by teammates, coaches, and opponents. I knew there were players out there who were better than I was, but I would have never said it. Every time I stepped onto a basketball court, I wanted to prove that I was the best on the court during those particular moments. Sometimes my intentions proved to be successful, other times not. Either way, people within the city knew I wasn't a chump, and I wasn't to be taken lightly when competing against me in the game of basketball. Minute after minute, hour after hour, day after day, I practiced. I was prepared for anything, or so I thought.

My junior year began. My class schedule was all set, we were considered to be a top program in the country, and all of a sudden, girls started falling out of the sky. Now don't get me wrong, I was never afraid to holla at girls... Well, I kind of was... Never mind. Either way, I had to step up to the plate and start playing the game. That was what being a student-athlete at a big time university was all about, right? At that age, it wasn't about power or money; it was about getting chicks—no ifs, ands, or buts about it. "Hunt or be hunted" was the motto we lived by. To top it all off, I met two of my best friends in the world that year, Jones and Wood. The term *wild children* doesn't accurately describe them; and then we had Hump, God's gift to women, or so he thought and was told by quite a few girls, we were told. The same holds true for the rest of my teammates. Reckless in their pursuit of the female persuasion would be an understatement. Sharks out of water, wolves on sheep, foxes in a hen house—you get the visuals.

I was a nerd compared to these guys. I studied a lot and didn't go out as much, but I was still a ninja. Get in, get out—the OG classic. Wood and I weren't as "bad" as the rest of the boys—not yet, anyway. We weren't devils, but we were far from angels. This is the year when a lot of individual learning took place. As usual, school wasn't a major concern. I knew I would do well if I remained focused and motivated. I was a leader in regards to academics on the team, and I wanted to keep it that way. I may not have been considered the best player on the team, but I definitely did not want to relinquish my title as one of the smartest and one of the hardest working individuals to grace the Notre Dame men's varsity basketball team.

Before the season officially began, I was a workhorse. I would go to class, study, eat, practice, study, study, and sleep. That was my daily routine. Nothing out of the ordinary except for this year, I actually had friends who liked to go out and girls wanted to go out with us. Time management and the willingness to say no became of vital importance. It's not that my teammates didn't want me to study, they just wanted to do things other than read and study a bunch of material that they would forget three minutes after the test was over anyway. Sometimes I would even go out and have fun with them. Actually, in an effort to maintain my sanity, it became a necessary evil. I was taking seventeen credits and was a bit overwhelmed, to be honest. Then I realized getting to know people was actually fun. I found out interacting with others is how you have an impact on their lives, positive or negative. My objective was to be a bright light even if there was darkness. Against all odds, I wanted people to know that with faith, hard work, and determination, anything could be done. I was not even really supposed to still be on that campus, but there I was... still standing.

The only "walk-on" who now was on scholarship had survived two coaches and was undoubtedly going to survive and maybe even thrive under the third. I was making history and did not even know it. The Notre Dame community started to recognize that when I was about twenty years old. Professors began commending me for my work ethic and outstanding scholastic achievements, stories were being written about me in the local newspaper, articles were being written about me in the school newspaper, and I was even voted to be "most likely to be the best boyfriend" by some student-initiated website. Reporters from TV stations were talking to me about my skill level and potential to play under a new coach, and I was receiving emails from students on the Notre Dame campus telling me how much of an inspiration I was to them. Oftentimes, the comments I would get from people would leave me speechless. I wasn't trying to impress, motivate, or inspire anyone. I was just doing me. That was all I knew how to do. I found out quickly that God allows people to see in others what He wants them to see. "Do your part," He says, "and I will do mine." Can't argue with that. Aside from all of the unintended inspiration and motivation that was going on, I was actually starting to have fun at school. That going out nonsense changed immediately, though, once the season began.

I was ecstatic. I was playing well and although I would argue with some of the guys on the team, it was never personal. We just expected the best out of each other and wanted to succeed as a unit. When people are competitive like we were, arguments are supposed to happen when you think someone is slacking off or not doing their absolute best to make themselves and the team better. I was the lone "walk-on" on the team, but that word was never mentioned—not around me, anyway. I was never introduced as CT the "walk-on." I was simply introduced as Charles, Chuck, or CT—nothing more, nothing less. I respected others and, in turn, I was respected. Things were going good. I was getting free basketball shoes, free basketball clothes, and I was actually playing well. In scrimmages, I would make more than significant contributions. This year, I knew I was going to play. Maybe not be a starter, but I was going to play. I had to. The first few games I did get more minutes than the previous years, but it was not what I expected, especially considering the fact that I was playing so well and was even told I was playing well by coaches on the staff. I wasn't having delusions of grandeur and just thought my game was nice; my thoughts and actions were being reaffirmed by coaches' statements.

Oh well, there was nothing more that I could do other than continue to play hard and be ready if my name and number were ever called. I did just that. Practices became my games, and I played every day as if the next day the game I loved the most would be taken away from me. I ran, I jumped, I scored, I handled the ball, I called out plays, I argued with teammates (even threatened a few), I did whatever necessary to make the team better. If that had to be my role, then so be it. I would be angry after most games because I knew that I was good enough and that I should have actually played. I didn't, though, so I had to train myself to not get so mad and down and out on myself.

Before the Serenity prayer became such a big deal, I had it in my room. My roommate, PJ, would see me pray every night, and I am sure he was wondering what I was praying about. Here it is: "God grant me the serenity to accept the things I cannot change, the courage to change the things I can change, and the wisdom to know the difference." If you can do something about your current situation, do something about it, but if you can't, don't worry about it. That prayer, along with my collegiate experiences, is why I do not worry, stress, or get all hot and bothered now. Life is too short. Boss up and do something about it or shut up—that is what I tell myself and that is what I am telling you.

Anyway, we were an extremely cohesive unit that year. If you saw one of us walk into a bar or club, rest assured within an hour you would see eleven more guys. A band of brothers we were. That is why we remained ranked for most of the season and actually won the Big East Championship. We lost to Mississippi State in the second round of the NCAA Tournament, and our record was 20-10. Notre Dame basketball was back on the map, and I was instrumental in its transition.

SENIOR YEAR

The summer before my senior was an absolute blast. I had made the Dean's List both semesters as a junior, we had won the Big East Championship, girls were loving me, my facial hair was actually starting to look like real facial hair, and did I mention that girls were loving me? This summer was a little bit different from the rest of the summers, though. Not only did I actually know who the coach was going be my senior year, but Swan (a teammate and excellent friend) and I were chosen to go to London, England, for a summer study abroad program. London was quite the experience. I was twenty-one years old and in another country with a bunch of other twenty-one-year-olds. My class schedule was busy, but not extremely difficult. I think the professors didn't make classes too difficult on purpose because they wanted students to know what is was like to live in a foreign place and actually learn the culture instead of studying twelve hours per day.

The experience was second to none. While Swan and I were there, we worked on our game, studied together, hung out together, and became very good friends. We learned the streets of London, we mingled with the rich people, we mingled with the poor people, and I even found time to play ball with some of the guys that played on a professional basketball team in London. My time there was phenomenal. While I was there, I traveled to Edinburgh, Scotland, and Paris, France.

Both places were wonderful but Scotland is, by far, the best place I have ever visited. Everything there was so gothic. The architecture of all of the buildings was exemplary. Almost every structure there had a gothic feel to it, like a king or queen graced the building with their presence at some point in time. The people were extremely accommodating, personable, and inquisitive. They were just as interested in my culture as I was in theirs. To share that experience with another human being is almost unfathomable to some, and I was doing it at the age of twenty-one. Through all of the adversity, I was still doing all right. I left London a more experienced student, smarter in world affairs, and with all A's and an A-, I think. Who really remembers, right? It was all about the experience.

Aside from my travels abroad, I actually knew who the basketball coach was going to be going into my senior year. It was almost too good to be true. It was not the time to become complacent, though. I learned a long time ago that complacency is an attitude far more dangerous than rage. In addition, I did not have any reason to be complacent. I still had something to prove. I wanted to prove to myself that I was major Division 1 material. I wanted to prove to myself that I was a Dean's List-level student. I wanted to prove to myself that I could make an actual difference in the lives of others.

So in customary fashion, I worked out harder than ever. A childhood friend and I shot between 700 and 1000 shots per day. Our workouts were grueling, but we improved every day. A day without some level of improvement was a wasted day. Time was of the essence, so neither one of us had the luxury of wasting a day. We ran, we lifted, and we worked on everything possible. "Comeback players of the year" was our slogan.

We would chant positive affirmations repeatedly throughout our workouts. It gave us a reason to believe. We knew that we were not alone in the world. Not only did we have each other to rely on and lean on for emotional support, but God was forever watching over us. There was nothing more that we could have asked for or even imagined. Knowing that the Creator was guiding and directing our paths was a powerful realization. The workouts were still hard, but at least we felt as if we had a purpose.

Before school actually began, I went back to campus to talk to Coach in an attempt to get guidance and clarification on my future. This is when I learned all about politics and the business of collegiate athletics. I walk into Coach's office and, as usual, I received a friendly and welcoming greeting. He told me to make sure I stayed motivated in school, and he knew how hectic my first semester as a senior was going to be since I had to manage seventeen credits again along with all of the basketball stuff. He congratulated me on a fine job the previous year and reiterated the importance of my leadership on the team. He also asked me what I envisioned for the program as a senior. I told him that I knew we were, once again, one of the top teams in the country, and not making the NCAA tournament would be an extreme disappointment to us all. I explained to him that I knew I was ready to contribute this year and that I would give it my all every day. I told him that I knew I was just as good as any of the other guards on the team, and I just wanted the opportunity to show it. He listened to everything I had to say and then told me something no normal twenty-one-year-old kid wants to hear.

He said, "Chuck, you are a great kid, a great student, and an excellent basketball player. There is only one problem. I have recruited another point guard who happens to be a McDonald's All-American, and I have to play him. Even if I did not want to, I would not have a choice."

He explained that if he didn't play the McDonald's All-American, upper level athletics administrators would be incensed, boosters would be outraged and potentially decrease funding, and future McDonald's All-Americans would not want to attend Notre Dame because of the fear of potentially not playing. I understood the logic behind it all, but it ripped me up inside. It was not fair to me that I would not even get the chance to prove myself. It was implied that no matter how hard I worked that year, how much I improved, how much of a contribution I could have made, it simply was not going to happen. At least he was honest with me. There was no room for misinterpretation.

Coach B talked so genuinely and sincerely that I could not be mad at him personally; I was only disappointed and angered by the situation. I told him that I truly appreciated his honesty and would handle the situation like a knight—with dignity, pride, class, and character. Internally, I could not help but think that I should have transferred to other schools when those opportunities presented themselves. I had to dispel those thoughts almost as quickly as they entered my mind because if I would not have, they would have eaten me alive. It hurt, though…real bad. I could have folded my hands and said, "I'm good. I had a good three-year run at it, but now it is time to call it quits and just be a student." I could have said that, but never in 100 billion years would I have ever said that. Instead, I focused on the positives and played the hand I was dealt because I knew that ultimately, I could still win.

The first semester of my senior year was one of the most grueling and intense periods of my life. My class schedule could not have been any more difficult, we were working out at least three to four hours per day, and I was only sleeping about three to four hours per night. In addition, I had to handle the temptation of going out on a more than frequent basis and deal with the peer pressure of hollering at as many chicks as humanly possible while maintaining my ninja/knight status. Life was hard, but it was fun. My days were different, but my routine stayed the same. Wake up, eat, class, practice, eat, study, study, study, eat, sleep, then back at it again the next day. I was completely exhausted. It was cool, though, because there were probably several hundred thousand people who would have traded places with me in a heartbeat. There were times of complete frustration, though. Despite what I was told by Coach earlier in the school year, I still oftentimes did not understand why I wasn't playing enough to make a significant contribution—one recognizable to the world and not just the Notre Dame family. There was nothing I could do, though, other than continue to work hard and always stay prepared, so that is what I did.

By the way, 9/11 happened during that semester. I won't go into details about it because none of us will ever forget that horrendous day. However, I will say that it entirely changed my prospective on how I viewed the world. I saw that Americans could come together and disregard racial, religious, societal, political, and ethnic tensions. I just wish that tragedy did not always have to precede such unity and harmony. I learned on that day that many of the things that might seem so devastating might not necessarily be so, and I also learned that even good things can be taken away in the blink of an eye. I learned to never take anything for granted and to be grateful for even the smallest of things that make you smile, because it can all be taken away from you before you know it.

Outside of basketball, everything was cool and got even better in early November. Being boys, some of us on the team would dare one of our teammates to go and get a girl's phone number to see if he could take her out on a date, a social outing, if you will. We were participating in what modern-day psychologists might call "social experimentation." The rules were simple. The girl had to be, on a scale of one to ten, between an eight and a ten; we did have reputations to keep, remember. That was it—make sure she was cute. If you were able to get her number, that was cool; if not, it wasn't the end of the world. It just meant that you had to step your mouthpiece game up. One night we were at a party, and it was my turn. The guys had to pick a girl for me. Keep in mind, on this night, many of us were way past drunk so the courage necessary to approach any girl was there. Anyway, they pointed to a girl, and she was gorgeous. No problem. Did I already mention to you that I couldn't even see straight at this point in the night? Well if I didn't, now you know.

I approached these two young ladies, and I couldn't remember which one Jones and Wood picked, so I just chose the one that I wanted. So I went through the normal nonsense that guys go through when they are trying to woo a girl, you know, ask her how she's doing, ask her what her name is, and blah blah blah. I did all of that, and she finally told me her name was Lana. I do not remember exactly what I said to her since I was in state of complete intoxication, but I am sure it was absolutely adorable. I talked to Lana for a few minutes, and some kind of way we ended up exchanging numbers. Good job to me, right? Wrong. I went back to Jones and Wood all excited, and they told me I picked the wrong girl. I didn't pick the wrong girl, I just didn't pick the one they told me to go get.

The night progressed, and I lost my phone. I almost had a complete panic attack because her number was stored in my phone. So me, being the dummy that I was, approached her again and told her that "I lost my phone with your number, so here is my number again." Wow. She looked at me like I was a big dummy. The thought probably going through her mind was, *Why would you give me your phone number again because you lost your phone?* Good question. I shouldn't have, but I just gave it to her anyway and walked away like an idiot. About an hour or so later, as we were getting ready to leave, one of my friends gave me my phone, and I was elated.

A few weeks went by, and I hadn't even called her. The thought never even crossed my mind, actually, until Jones said something about it. We were in my room talking about our upcoming basketball trip to Hawaii, and he asked if I ever called the chick from that one night. I sure had not, but I called her that night, and it was the beginning of my first real relationship. I had a girlfriend in high school my senior year, but it only lasted for about nine months, so it's not the same, I don't think. That relationship was more of a teenage love affair.

The team left for Hawaii, and it was a wonderful experience. We had fun, and we worked hard. Prior to that trip, I had not experienced anything like that. Clear blue skies, crystal clear water, and beautiful Hawaiian girls all over the place who loved us simply because we were athletes who didn't live in Hawaii. Our week in Honolulu was amazing; and to top it all off, we were crowned champions of the Hawaii Pacific Thanksgiving Classic. I was even given the opportunity to play. I could not have asked for anything more.

During my time there I began talking to Lana quite a bit and had an inclination that she might stick around for a while. She was gorgeous, fun, smart, ambitious, kind of corny, but I liked it. I didn't want her to be too "hood." We made a good team. We were different in so many ways, yet we were alike. I did not actually get the chance to go out with her until she came back home for Christmas break. She attended a university in another state, so from the beginning of our friendship, we only had the opportunity to see each other on a monthly basis, if that. Christmas break was fun, though, and on our third date, I had to play nurse. The team had a party, she came along, and tried to drink and keep up with the big boys. I thought, *That was the wrong move, baby girl.* She handled it like a soldier, though, until about 2:00 a.m. We got back to our room, and she and Jones were throwing up like I have never seen, and all I could think was, *What the f*** is going on here?* I barely knew how to take care of myself, so I knew it was going to be an adventure trying to take care of two drunken dummies. I ran back and forth in an effort to make sure both of them were okay.

Jones started to feel better, so I decided it was time to take Lana home. We got to her house, and her parents weren't there. If it would have been up to me, I would have just walked her about two steps into her house, put her on the couch, and walked out. That didn't happen. She asked me to take her upstairs and put her in the bed. All I could think was, *How will I ever explain what I was doing upstairs if her parents come home?* I picked her up, ran upstairs, put her in the bed, made sure she was okay, and then I left. I made it out before her parents got home. She had the worst hangover the next day. It made me laugh, actually. It was about time it happened to someone other than me. After that day, the feeling that I was going to stick around for a while was getting stronger and stronger.

Christmas break was going well until I went home for a few days. During my visit, I saw my future and life all flash before my eyes. If you recall, I told you how tenuous my relationship was with my dad throughout high school and into college. Well, it almost all came to a tragic end a couple of days before Christmas. I truly do not remember what pushed me over the edge that day, but if Jones had not have called my phone at the precise moment that he did, I would probably be writing this story from a jail cell and not from my 2500-plus square foot home.

All I really remember was my dad yelling at my mom, and I lost it. I am not sure what he was yelling about; he could have just been excited while telling a funny joke for all I know. Either way, it was enough to cause an out-of-body experience. I was sitting in my room reading when I heard the commotion. I got up and before he could say anything to me, I went on an absolute tirade. I explained to him, in no uncertain terms, that if I ever even thought that he even dreamed about hitting my mom again, I would kill him and wait for the cops to come. I told him that I would beat him to the point of near death, let him regain consciousness, and beat him again until his entire existence was eradicated. I have no idea where such courage and venom came from, but it was there and was not going to go away easily. He began to approach me and as he did, I grabbed two extremely large butcher knives and begged him to continue moving forward. At this time, Mom and my sister were in a complete state of shock, I am sure. They were unable to say anything other than "Please put the knives down and go into your room."

I did not put the knives down, but I did go to my room, but not before explaining to him that if he took one step into my room, I was going to cut him into tiny pieces and feed him to the cats. I sat in my room infuriated and not knowing what to expect. He told me that he had called the police and that they were going to make me get out of his house. My answer to him was if the cops walked into my room, they better come in shooting because if they don't, more cops were going to have to carry them out in body bags as well.

I heard him begin to walk closer to my door; as I got up to meet him, my phone rang. Lo and behold, it was Jones—God's angel for me—at that particular moment. We talked for over three hours that night. *About what?* you ask. I have no idea. Whatever it was, it calmed me down and made it so that I did not make the biggest mistake of my life by killing the man who was partially responsible for bringing me into this world. So Jones, I say to you thank you. You saved my life and did not even know it. God works in mysterious ways, and that night you were an angel sent from heaven. There is no other way to describe it, and I truly believe it. So again, thank you for being there for me on that night. You are appreciated.

The night ended through sincere apologies from all parties involved. I did not go to jail, the police did not have to arrest me, and everyone remained alive. It all ended okay, considering it could have been a lot worse. I called Lana and, once again, the universe was in balance; she made everything all right.

We were well into the second semester of my senior year, and after about six months of talking to Lana and visiting each other, my mom asked if I was still dating her. It dawned on me that we were still dating, and I actually liked her. That semester was like a cakewalk compared to the rest of my college career. I only had two or three classes at that point, I had a wonderful girlfriend, we were doing well as a team, and I was finally having fun. I would sometimes still get down and out about not playing as much as I thought I should have, but I had learned how to self-manage my emotions at that point, and the lengths of time that I was upset were much shorter than in the past. I was no longer a little boy, and I knew throwing a temper tantrum was not the right response. The season progressed, and although I didn't see Lana as much as I would have liked, we talked every night before I went to bed. I looked forward to talking to her because I knew that no matter how bad my day was, she would figure out a way to make it seem as if everything would be okay. She was turning into my princess in shining armor. I thought I was going to be the one to rescue a person, but it seemed to be the other way around. Having her around even made the not playing in every game more bearable.

As the season continued, we were getting better and better and knew that we would once again hear our name called to be a part of the NCAA Tournament. We were a part of something special, a select group of individuals who would be afforded the opportunity to play to win a national championship. One of my teammates had a tattoo that read "Truly Blessed," and we were exactly that. We finished the regular season and, unfortunately, we did not repeat as Big East Champions that year. It was cool because, as we anticipated, we were chosen to be in the field of 64. With a third consecutive twenty-win season in one of college basketball's toughest conferences, the selection committee had no choice but to select us as NCAA Tournament participants. We traveled to Greenville, South Carolina, to play our first game against the University of North Carolina at Charlotte. We played well and won 82-63.

As a unit, we were working efficiently and had our eyes set on our next opponent: the Duke Blue Devils. We knew they were going to be tough competition, but we also believed in ourselves enough to know that we could beat them. The competition was intense. Players were arguing with each other, fouls were being handed out to both teams, and we were winning the entire game until about the last five or six minutes. All of a sudden, it was like Coach K told his players to not miss another shot, because I don't think they did. When the final horn sounded, we were losing 77-84, and just like that, my basketball career at the University of Notre Dame was over.

Uncontrollable tears of sadness overwhelmed me. I, along with almost everyone else on the team, was not crying because we lost, although that was a part of it, but it was more so the fact that the brotherhood had officially ended. A group of boys had come together with a common objective: to win a national championship. We fell short of our ultimate goal, but we learned so many things, gained so many life experiences, and shared so many memories during that quest for excellence. We had grown so close to each other over the past few years and to know that it was over was heartbreaking. We would all go on to be successful in whatever field that we ultimately ended up going into, but we all knew that it was not going to be the same. We understood that we would never have the same camaraderie with coworkers, bosses, and unknowns who did not fight the battle with us as collegiate athletes. Those people would be friends, but they would never be a part of our fellowship, our society, our brotherhood on the Notre Dame basketball team. It was a sad day to say the least, but I would do it all over again.

Once basketball season ended, we had our end-of-the-year basketball banquet. This was the time of the year when coaches and players got up on stage in front of a few thousand people to present awards and say a few nice things about the team. I had the privilege of talking about a few of my teammates and taking a trip down memory lane. It was beautiful and an experience that I will forever cherish. I also learned a few things about my journey at Notre Dame as well. I was informed that I was the only basketball player in Notre Dame's storied history to begin his collegiate career as a "walk-on" and play for three different coaching staffs in a four-year period. Many people would approach me and say that was a hell of an accomplishment, and while I would humbly accept their congratulatory remarks, I was just doing me; and along the way, I wrote myself into Notre Dame history. During that banquet, I was also presented with the Notre Dame Knute Rockne Student-Athlete of the Year Award for having the highest grade point average on the team. I was honored to have such an award bestowed upon me, and later that year, there would be more to come.

After the banquet was over and there were not any more official basketball-related functions, the pressure and anxiety of what to do next started to build. Would I try to play professional basketball overseas, would I try to get a job in corporate America, would I work for the Federal Bureau of Investigation or the Central Intelligence Agency, would I go to graduate school? These were the myriad of questions I would have to answer on an almost daily basis to friends, family, and sometimes the media. I was more fortunate than some because I had options. My grades were decent, I had a strong network of advocates working on my behalf, I was focused, and I had God on my side. I had worked hard and prepared myself for almost anything, so the certainty of uncertainty was appealing to me. Not knowing where life was going to take me was an adventure in and of itself. I continued to lift weights and work on my game because I was not ready to give up basketball just yet. I studied for the GRE and GMAT just in case I wanted to go to graduate school, and I began filling out job applications just in case the first two options were not really options. While I was preparing for everything simultaneously, I received a call from, in my opinion, the most prestigious agency in the world. I will let you use your imagination to figure it out, though. I will give you a hint: it has three letters in it. Was it the CIA, FBI, NSA, TBS, TNT, or ESPN? Makes you go, "Hmm," huh?

Anyway, I was not sure I wanted to pursue such a profession. To me, basketball was still an option. As usual, I talked to people who I considered wiser than myself and asked for their advice. The answers varied so much that consulting them actually made the decision harder. Some people advocated working for the government, some said go get a graduate degree, and others said try to basketball professionally. I was lost in a maze with no clear direction on where to turn. I just had to give time more time. As the school year was nearing its end, I was surprised to be, once again, nominated for a high-level award, the NAACP Senior of the Year. I knew a lot of people at the time, but I didn't think that I had made big enough waves to be nominated for something like that. It was an honor to be nominated, and I was sure that I was not going to win. I was only a student who happened to play basketball. At that particular award ceremony, other awards were giving to students, but the NAACP Senior of the Year Award was bestowed upon me. I humbly accepted the award and thanked all of those who voted for me. I still do not know how I won that award but, hey, it is what it is. Divine intervention at its best, I guess.

After that award, I was also informed that I was chosen as an Arthur Ashe Jr. Sports Scholars Award recipient—not bad for a kid from Flint who was not even supposed to be there. I could just imagine all of the haters turning over in their graves, and I loved it. To me, it was a great feeling to do what people said I could not do. Once the awards ceremonies all ended and school was officially over, it was time to make a decision. Was it going to be to pursue a career in basketball or work for the government? At least I had narrowed the choices to two.

LEARN TO FLY

College life was over, and it was time to move on. I had rewritten the ND history books, I had a positive impact on the lives of others, I won a few awards in the process, and I had a wonderful girlfriend. I had to forget about all past accomplishments and start to achieve more. I still was not sure what to do about life at this point, but I had a few things in the works. I was undergoing a complete background investigation by the federal government, and I chose to pursue a career in basketball by attending several professional exposure camps throughout the United States. I went back home to Flint and enlisted the services of one of my very best friends and mentors, Martin. Martin owned his own business, played ball in college, and played professional basketball overseas for many years. He was knowledgeable, fun to be around, well connected, and a great teacher. He trained and taught me things that would prove to be extremely successful in my quest to be recognized as someone with professional athlete potential. Not only was he a great teacher in regards to basketball, but he also taught me several life lessons that will remain with me until my number is called to go to heaven.

My confidence level increased under his guidance, and there was absolutely no fear of failure. He gave suggestions as to some of the best camps in the country and based on his advice, I traveled to Florida, Indiana, Virginia, New Jersey, DC, and Ohio (those are the ones I can remember) in an effort to showcase my talent and get a deal to play ball professionally. I entered many camps as a relatively unknown name, but I didn't leave any of them that way. I was consistently rated as one of the top guards at every camp that I attended, and I made the all-star team at every camp, except one. I was playing at a high enough level, and it was just a matter of time before a deal was done, and I knew it. I received calls to play ball in London and Portugal, and my journey to be considered a professional athlete was complete.

I only practiced for a short period of time before I did everything but break my ankle in half. I tore virtually every ligament in my right ankle, and that was that; my season was over. Good thing I had the educational background and ability to pursue other options because I definitely needed them. Sure enough, the option to work for the government manifested itself.

Approximately eight months after I graduated college, I began my first real job. The technology, the levels of intelligence, the secrecy, and overall aura of the place was everything I imagined it would be, plus more. The things you see on TV are not nearly as sophisticated as what the government really has. I learned skills on the inside that would get any human being on the outside locked up. Skills like the art of elicitation, effective questioning, negotiation techniques, and in-depth analysis. I also enjoyed improving my capabilities in the art of storytelling.

It was quite the experience to be an integral part of such an organization. I participated in activities, heard stories, analyzed cases, strategically planned operations, and experienced things that most people will never experience in a lifetime. It was an amazing ride.

I did learn, however, that nothing is what it seems. I learned that there are some people in this world whose ultimate goal in life is to manipulate others and trick the system. They have hate in their hearts and will do whatever it takes to stop you from breathing—case in point, September 11, 2001. It was truly an enlightening experience to read about these people, hear them speak, and understand their ideological and religious reasons for planning and executing such acts of brutality on innocent people. According to them, the West was far from innocent. It was Allah's calling for them to wage jihad ("holy war") against such ignorance and restore harmony and balance in the world. The arrogance of the Western world would be our downfall and lead to complete annihilation of the human race. It was a good thing that my childhood desensitized me to such malicious acts; otherwise, I do not think I would have been able to survive in such a world.

Being the ambitious kid that I was, I decided it was absolutely necessary to begin a master's degree program right away. My roommate, EJ, advised against it, but I would not listen. It was necessary, or so it seemed, to gain a masters of science in strategic intelligence since I was working for the federal government. Gaining that type of degree at such an early age would allow me to write my own ticket. In my infinite wisdom, that is what I thought. I had just graduated from the University of Notre Dame, had recognizable talent as a professional basketball player, and was working for one of the most prestigious government agencies in the world. I did not want to hear anything from anyone. Arrogance was beginning to set in, but I was humbled rather quickly when that program started and life started throwing more curve balls at me. It seemed natural to be overwhelmed, so working fifteen hours per day and going to graduate school shouldn't have been a big deal. I was completely wrong. The workload associated with a master's of science in strategic intelligence was as hard as it sounded. I quickly learned that extensive work experience was a necessity to succeed with minimal difficulty in such a program. I was the youngest and the most inexperienced, but I was willing to learn nonetheless. It was complete baptism by fire.

My ankle was beginning to get better so, once again, I was at the gym every day. Life was a complete firestorm. I was working approximately fifteen hours per day, working out for about three hours per day, and doing homework and reading for about two hours per night. Do the math and, yes, it is absolutely true that I was only sleeping about four hours per night. I was learning, though. I was becoming extremely proficient at my day job and being a top-rated student and employee felt natural. I was starting to meet many people at the gym because of basketball, and I was beginning to enjoy being the go-to guy at work. Aside from that, I met some of the most influential people in my life while living and working in Virginia. Talli was like a big brother, and his wife was just as helpful; EJ was like another brother; Shad was like my little brother;, and Kurt was a mentor and friend. I observed their actions, asked questions, answered questions, and tried to be a positive light in their lives.

Those are the non-work friends who had such a lasting, positive impression on me. Talli is one of the hardest working individuals I have ever met. He was extremely helpful to younger children and did his absolute best to teach them the game of basketball. He was the epitome of the word teacher. EJ was a cool cat; he had a swag about him that many people his age didn't have. He was smart, ambitious, fun, athletic, and he inspired me to do better. I tried every day to keep up with him and gain his approval and respect. A hard guy to impress, but I think I was able to do it. Shad was like the little brother I never had; he was feisty, sarcastic, rude at times, loving all the time, inquisitive, and a lover of basketball. He looked up to me and EJ like we really were his older brothers. He wanted to be like us so bad that he, in a way, mythologized us. He would ask questions until he understood and was never afraid to learn. It is not every day that you run across a group of genuine people who care about your welfare and pray at night that you succeed in life. I came across those types of people within four months of living in VA, and that was just at the gym.

I also met a phenomenal group of people at work who inspired me to do better. My first boss, Darlein, was absolutely wonderful. She trusted my judgment and gave me tasks to accomplish with little to no supervision. I was with her for a couple of months before intense training began. She was a single mother and the same fire, desire, and love that she used to raise her daughter was evident in the workplace. She was professional, helpful, thoughtful in her ways, and extremely passionate about her job. She made decisions without fear of consequences, spoke her mind about issues of importance, was inquisitive and always sought first to understand before seeking to be understood. Darlein taught me valuable life and work lessons. She was the first person in my professional career who wholeheartedly believed in me. She told me on an almost daily basis that I was a special kid and was going to make it one day. She would say, "Charles, no matter how hard it is, or how hard it gets, I want you to look at yourself in the mirror during those tough times and say to yourself, with absolute conviction, that 'I am going to make it.'" I was only twenty-three years old at the time and was unaware of what the world had in store for me. In customary motherly fashion, she saw something in me that I did not even see in myself and felt it necessary to speak words of encouragement, faith, and love over me. I have not seen or spoken to Darlein in quite some time, but she was an inspiration to me. Her words of encouragement resonated with me and reaffirmed my faith in humanity. She was a blessing sent from above, and to her I will be forever thankful.

Aside from Darlein, there were seven other friends that I met early in my government career that I have to mention: Kailan, Michele, Tiffiny, Brett, Stephanie, Tarq, and Lynn. These seven individuals were and are intelligent, fun, outgoing, ambitious, motivated, humble, and sincere. I learned professional and personal lessons from them all. We were all about the same age, experiencing the same things, and handling the same types of issues. Although we all grew up differently, we were now all running the same race and trying to accomplish common objectives. For me, seeing other young people who were just as motivated to succeed in life was refreshing.

The only problem was that I did not get a chance to hang out with them too much because I was too focused and doing too much. Sleeping so few hours because of working such long hours and keeping up with schoolwork was starting to wear on me. My body was beginning to give out and I could feel it. I was unaware of how to appropriately handle life at this point, so I handled it the best way I knew how: say nothing and deal with it. I just continued to do what I was doing. I really did not have any other alternatives. I could have just quit school, but I did not think that would be the best decision. I could have cut back on my work hours, but I wanted to stand out in a crowd. I wanted my name to be mentioned by itself when the bosses were talking about the "young talent." I could have stopped working out at night, but then I might not have been ready if I would have received another call to go play basketball internationally.

Ostensibly, there was nothing that I could have stopped doing to make my life easier. I maintained a positive relationship with them all and became good friends with them, but it could have been a lot better. It was my fault, though, that I did not know how to do it. So I apologize to them now for not doing my part to make things even better than they were. I was a kid trying to make something out of nothing. The worse part about all of this was the fact that my relationship with Lana was negatively affected. I was never home, I was not making enough money at the time to go and visit her like I would have liked, and she was in medical school so she could not leave whenever she wanted. I would be so tired and sleepy some nights when I finally got home that I would only talk to her for about ten minutes or so before my body shut down and made me go to sleep. So what did I do to make it all better? I bought a dog, a Boston terrier, and I named him Irish.

Irish had the unwanted pressure of doing whatever necessary to make my life more fun and enjoyable. EJ bought a dog too, so now we had two puppies running around the apartment. It was fun, but it made my life a little harder. I forgot that you had to feed dogs, take them outside, bathe them, give them shots, take them to the vet, and actually play with them. I figured since there were two of them running around, they would be able to do all of that stuff for each other. Wishful thinking, because that was definitely not the case. I considered giving Irish away within the first week for several reasons: my allergies were killing me, he did not want to play, I had to feed him out of my hand, and he slept and acted like a cat instead of a dog.

Chase was the worst dog in the history of dogs for a while. He played too much, barked too loud, ate everything, did the number-one and number-two whenever and wherever he felt like it, and did not listen. After a couple of months of training and patience, things began to get better. I was still extremely busy, but Irish and Chase were doing a good job of keeping me happy. Their unconditional love and joy that came through every day or night when I came home were more than welcome. What is even better is the fact that a dog, not a human, taught me how to be patient, how to slow down and enjoy the simple things, and how to forget about bad things as soon as they are over. Irish truly was turning into my best friend, and eight years later, he is still here with me... loving life.

Although Irish was exceeding all expectations, life was still very difficult. My youngest sister was putting my parents through hell, school was killing me, work was beginning to get repetitive, my body was beginning to break down from working out and playing ball so much, and things with Lana were still shaky. I loved her with all of my heart, but was unaware of how much longer we could sustain a long-distance relationship. At this point, EJ really began to recognize that life was wearing me down and would often advise that I slow down and be careful. I would hear his suggestions, but not act accordingly. He was in school at the time, too, so he felt my pain. We were leading similar lives, and I think his suggestions to me were also his suggestions to himself—many of which he also did not follow. We were young, invincible, and had to do everything all at once. I was in a complete state of confusion.

To the outside world, things were going well, but internally, I was melting away. The job had become more than monotonous, and even though I was ranked as a top employee in our particular functional unit, I felt as if my talents, brain cells, and overall personality were getting worse. So instead of complaining, I figured I should do something about it. I was in a graduate program, but it was not fulfilling me like I initially anticipated, plus it was brought to my attention that a masters of science degree in strategic intelligence would not translate into a higher salary or even be well-recognized outside of the government world. I had a dilemma and was unsure of how to proceed. I knew that I did not want to do government work forever, especially if what I was currently doing was any indication of how things would be in the future, but I also did not want to simply exit the program without any legitimate reasons.

Although the work was difficult, I was doing well, and the thought of stopping something before it was complete did not sit well with me. However, I was not stupid enough to let pride overcome logical thought. I refused to remain unhappy at such an early age, and I began contemplating if leaving government work and pursuing an MBA or law degree was a suitable alternative. I consulted former coaches, close friends, relatives, former academic counselors, and former professors and decided that an MBA would be the most useful to me.

I decided that I would apply to quite a few nationally ranked and recognized MBA programs across the country. On my list were schools such as Florida, UT-San Antonio, UT-Austin, Notre Dame, Georgia, and California, to name a few. I maintained my daily routine, continued in my current degree program and prepared to take the (what I considered to be impossible to pass) GMAT. I studied for a few weeks, took the test, and did decently well. I did not do as well as I probably could or should have if I would have enrolled in a GMAT preparation course prior to taking the test, but it was an afterthought at that point. I had done well enough to apply to the schools that I was interested in, so I was going to do it.

I sent applications to schools that I figured would be a good fit for me and began playing the waiting game. A few days went by, and I began to call school to get a status update as to whether or not they received my application packet. In customary fashion, however, life threw me another curve ball. I finished speaking to a graduate admissions representative in regards to my application materials, and he told me that he would have an answer for me in a couple of weeks. I was fine with that answer. I just liked to know what's going on.

A few minutes after finishing that call, my cell phone rang again. It was my mother calling. If you recall, I am from Flint, Michigan, one of the most dangerous cities in America. I could tell by the sound of her voice that something was deeply troubling her, and I automatically assumed the worst. She began to tell me that a group of girls tried to carjack my sister, but she escaped and nothing bad happened. She told me I needed to do something about it. What was I to do? I was about 600 miles away from home and was oblivious to the lifestyle that my sister was leading at the time. No one motivated me to try to make a better life for myself. I did that with the help and guidance from God. As a result, I figured my sister would have to make up her own mind to want to help herself before I could do anything. I had enough problems at the time, so taking on another was not something I was interested in doing. Ultimately, I told my mom I would talk to her.

I did not even have the opportunity to call her because she called me immediately after I finished talking to Moms. She told me the story, began to cry, and asked if she could come and live with me. What was I to say? I always put family first. I had no choice in the matter. She talked and explained to me how she wanted to make a better life for herself and be afforded the opportunity for a fresh start. I listened as she vented and told her that she could come and live with me—no worries. I figured that if I were in a position of need, she would be the first to help me. I bought a plane ticket that day and flew to Michigan the next. We packed her brand new Equinox with as much stuff as we could and began the ten-hour journey back to Virginia. During the drive, I knew that my life had completely changed. I could barely take care of myself, but decided to take on the task of being responsible for another human life. She was not a baby, but she was still my sister, so it was up to me to make sure that everything in her world was good. I jumped and prayed that I would learn to fly on my way down. That was the first time I made a such a drastic leap of faith, but I had to believe, and it definitely would not be the last jump I made.

During the drive, I talked to her and let her know that things would be different. While I would not act like a father figure, I would hold her to higher standards and make her accountable for her actions. I explained to her that I would do everything in my power to make her life comfortable as long as I felt as if she was trying. I expected her to work, or go to school. We agreed that if she enrolled in an undergraduate program, she would not have to pay as many bills because of her efforts to excel in a scholastic environment. However, if she chose not to go to school by the beginning of the spring semester, she would have to pay bills and make a financial contribution. There was no confusion, no miscommunication, and no misunderstandings. Ten hours later, we were at the apartment in Virginia. Her world had changed, and so had mine. Unbeknownst to her and everyone in my family, I called every graduate program to which I had applied and withdrew my applications. I was back at square one. My plans had completely changed. Not only did I feel responsible for another person, but I was beginning to question my potential and wonder about the future. I had jumped and learned how to fly on my way down, but I had no idea of which direction to fly.

Again, externally I was doing fine. I was still in graduate school, work was going well, and I was playing well in basketball leagues and camps, hoping to get a breakthrough. Internally, there was a struggle between me and myself. The man I was was having difficulties trying to figure out how to be the man that I wanted to become. I was teaching and being taught at the same time. Bridging the gap from what is to what should be is not as easy as people think. It is a testament of a person's will and desire to succeed when one can recognize that something is seemingly impossible and yet be determined to make it otherwise.

I was in the process of doing research for a thesis on Chinese affairs when life hit me again. *What the f****, I thought. One evening EJ came home and told me that he was about to buy a house. We both had talked about it in the past, but I did not think it was going to happen so fast. I was happy for both of us because I knew God was in our house. We were both tithing and/or donating to charities and trying to live right, so at some point I knew things were going to get better. God had given us both the opportunity to be stewards over small things such as our dogs and our apartment; now He was going to give us the chance to take on bigger challenges. My only problem was that I was not making enough money to live on my own just yet. Consequently, my happiness for him was derailed by my own fears. *How will I handle the situation?* I asked. The only logical answer and the only method that had worked to date was prayer, so that is what I did. I began to pray and ask God to guide me in whatever direction He saw fit, and I would be willing to follow. I knew that I was going to have to get a house for me and Tiana anyway because two guys, a girl, and two dogs in a 1400 square foot apartment seemed to be a little too small for comfort. I just did not anticipate looking for a house so quickly.

I began to strategize and figure out alternative ways to make money. Although work was monotonous and I was working ridiculous hours, I was still gaining valuable life experiences, and I knew it. I was gaining skills in the art of effective questioning, and I was becoming better at analyzing all types of situations. I was also going to school for free, and if I switched units, that would no longer be an option. I was starving, though, and I knew I had to do something to make my life and my sister's life easier. A month went by, and EJ found and closed on a house. Reality was here, and I had to do something. Talking about things was no longer a viable option, I had to make a move. I called a former colleague who also worked in the industry and asked if she could pass my résumé along to someone in the unit I was most interested in. Within four hours of talking to her, my phone rang, and an interview was scheduled for the next day. I knew this was divine intervention. The new unit that I was most interested in was completely different from my current position because it included analytical work as well as field operations. I did not tell anyone in my current unit that I was looking for another position because I did not want to rock the boat unnecessarily.

The next day, I went to the interview during my lunch break. I was not positive that I would get the position because I was the youngest candidate and I had the fewest years of experience, but I knew that I interviewed well. Two days later, I get a call from the boss telling me that not only were they offering me the new position, but I would also get a $40,000 increase in pay. When you do well with the little things God asks you to do, He will bless you with more than you can ask or imagine. I was going to have to withdraw from the graduate program if I took the job, but I knew something better was waiting for me. I learned many years ago that God never closes one door without giving you the keys to another. I was able to look at a different echelon of houses and, fortunately, I was not going to have start robbing people to make a way for me and my family.

I was ecstatic and knew that God and his angels were really watching over me. I accepted the position and told my current boss that I was taking a new position in an effort to enhance my skill level and aid in my personal and professional growth. While he was sad to see me go, he understood my situation and wished me the best. Within a few weeks of accepting the position, I found a house that my sister and I both liked, and I put an offer on it. The seller accepted the offer, and I would own my first home at the age of twenty-four. Instead of panicking, I stepped up to the free throw line, with ice in my veins, and calmly delivered. My parents drove to Virginia to assist with the move, and I began my new position right after Thanksgiving. That holiday was right on time because I had many reasons to be thankful. I had health, strength, my own house, my own money, and I was about to embark on a new journey that was sure to be full of surprises.

As I mentioned, I had to withdraw from the graduate program that I was in, but it was all for the good because I had a lot of on-the-job learning that was going to occupy a substantial amount of my time. For the first few months, I was in a location conducting unclassified analysis before I was able to move into my preferred position. In January of the next year, I began a journey that most twenty-four-year-old kids only read about. Once again, I had to jump and learn how to fly on my way down. Was I ready? Absolutely. I did not have a choice.

FOCUS: THE SHARPER IT IS, THE SHARPER YOU ARE

I was now working in a classified environment, and discretion was imperative. I learned rather quickly to only discuss things with people who had a need to know that information. I began to study my counterparts and tried to learn their personalities as quickly as possible. My previous position had taught me many things even though I was not aware of it at the time, but I now had the skill of analyzing and reading people and their behavioral patterns in a precise and accurate manner. This skill/talent was recognized by my new coworkers and bosses in a short amount of time. I was unaware of what was being said, but I was hopeful that references pertaining to me were positive in nature. Being the youngest and only black person in the unit, I felt as if I had to prove my worth, and I was determined to do so.

During the first few months of work, I went to an assortment of training classes, and I was acquiring skills that would allow me to protect myself and loved ones regardless of the situation. When I began, I was advised that it would take about a year before I would catch on to everything. I would nod my head in agreement, all the while thinking that whoever said progress had to be a slow process did not know me. I focused on the tasks at hand, learned how to use a variety of analytical tools at my disposal, and became proficient in my job. I was well versed in everything that I had to participate in and was not afraid to ask and/or answer questions. I understood the data and unfortunately, began to recognize that the world was much more dangerous than it seemed. I still was not doing exactly what I wanted to do, but I knew I had to build a strong foundation before venturing off into other worlds. I was equipped with the necessary repertoire to move forward in a progressive manner. Some people in the office were upset that I had the opportunity to attend so many training classes but, as the Bible says, you have not because you ask not. I worked many hours, and when a class came up that I thought would be beneficial, I asked to go. More often than not, my request was accepted.

While I was working, I still had it in my mind that I wanted to play basketball professionally overseas. I knew I was still good enough but needed the right opportunity. So as usual, I would work out after work. I was not in school at this point, so my evenings were free. I would get home before dark and hit the gym. I would lift weights and work on my game as if I were still in college. I also decided to attend more elite-level exposure camps. Although I had to pay for them, I was willing to accept the risk. My focus and passion were frightening. My sister would ask me how I did it every day. Even before I understood Nietzsche's proverb of "A man who has a why can bear almost any how," I was living it. I wanted to prove to myself that I could reach an elite level of athletic excellence once again. I wanted to give my family a better life, and I thought basketball was the only way to do it. I was making pretty good money working for the government, but basketball was still my first love, and there was nothing that could come even remotely close to replacing it.

I traveled to New Jersey to participate in a camp and played extremely well. My team had the best record during the week, and I was rated as the number-three guard there. I did not complain because I went in unrated, and the guards who were ranked number one and number two were both on my team and were deserving of such rankings. Number two had a short stint in the

NBA and the other, last I heard, was getting paid extremely well to play in Italy. I left camp floating on cloud 9000. I was not sure when I was going to get the call, but I knew it was going to come. After almost two months of waiting, I knew I had to face reality and accept the fact that I was not going to get an offer to play anywhere. I had not given up on myself, but I needed to move forward and prepare for the future.

I decided I would go to school to get my MBA. I applied to schools in the Virginia/DC area because they were close to my job and I would be able to attend classes on a part-time basis. I was accepted and began my quest for an advanced level degree... again. I was not even one month into the program when my cell phone rang on a Monday evening. An agent from Portugal was on the other end of the phone line telling me that he would like to represent me because a team in Portugal was requesting my services by Friday of the same week. I thought, *Wow. Thanks for the advanced notice, sir.* The timing of the phone call could not have come at a worse time. I had just started a graduate program for the second time and, to make it worse, I paid for the first semester out-of-pocket. I was attending a private university so if I would have left, I would have lost a substantial amount of money. In addition, my mortgage at that time was $2100 per month. Mind you, due to my current profession, I was extremely analytical and by no means would I make any emotional and/or illogical decisions. The spontaneous, emotional decision-making side of me was nonfunctional. I had to weigh the advantages and disadvantages of making such a move.

I had to consider how it would affect me professionally, how it would affect my sister, and how it would affect my family. This was not going to be an easy choice. There was a certain amount of money that was absolutely necessary if I was going to make it work. I was willing to take a drastic pay cut from my current salary, but I was going to need at least $2600 per month to make it work. That monetary amount would have been enough to pay the mortgage and my car note. The agent's response was that the highest offer was $2200 per month. I talked to my sister about it, and she was all for it. She advised that I should do it and she would figure out how to take care of things in my absence. It was a noble gesture, but not likely to end positively. She was working at a hair salon at the time, and if anything would have went wrong, she was not financially secure enough to handle it. I could not ask my parents to help because they did not have the money, and I was making just as much as they were making as a couple. I was making almost three times as much as the team was offering me; and although my goal of being recognized as a professional-level athlete had once again been realized, I had to respectfully decline. Economically and logically, it did not make sense to make such a drastic move for such a small monetary value. Sure, I would have been playing ball in Portugal and gaining more international experience, but who was to say I would have went over there and stayed injury free. Sports can be taken away from someone in the blink of an eye, and I knew it could because it had already happened to me. One thing I knew that could never be taken away from me was a strong educational background and knowing that I did what was necessary to take care of a family member who needed me in her life, even if only for a season.

If I would have known what the future had in store for me, maybe my decision would have been different. I am not a prophet, however, so predicting the future was not something that I was particularly adept at with any degree of certainty. Either way, the decision was made, and there was no turning back the hands of time to have a chance at changing my mind. Even knowing what I know now, I would have made the same decision because although things did not ultimately turn out the way that I wanted them to, taking care of family is always the most important.

Time was not going to stand still, and neither was I. Therefore, moving forward with a positive attitude and healthy outlook on life was my only alternative. I remained enrolled in my graduate degree program, continued to learn at work, and thanked God for giving me such opportunities. There was no reason for me to feel sad or think about the past when I knew there was so much potential for greatness and awe-inspiring moments in my future. A few weeks, maybe even an entire month went by, and life was going fairly well. I was doing well in school and paying bills on schedule; my relationship with Lana was doing much better, and my faith was strong. Just when things were going great Murphy's Law kicked in. Everything that could go wrong did.

If you recall from an earlier chapter, I explained how my mom and sister's relationship was strained. It was like watching two hungry pit bulls trying to coexist in the same cage—not a pretty sight. Her lack of respect for others and herself had a debilitating effect on our relationship. She began listening to uneducated, unmotivated, and manipulative people who did not have her best interests at heart and only wanted her to struggle in the same manner that they were struggling. I am not exactly sure how she allowed the devil to take over, but a spirit of envy and hate began to manifest itself in her life.

Tiana was no longer Tiana at this point. Her alter ego, "Stacy," had taken over, and it was apparently her goal to wreak havoc and cause complete destruction and chaos in the lives of others. I previously mentioned that she decided pursuing a collegiate level education was not a good option and instead opted to work in a hair salon. There is absolutely nothing wrong with working in a hair salon, so do not misunderstand what I am saying. I am simply trying to relate to you that her struggle was unnecessary. I explained to her on more than one occasion that if she enrolled in a university and pursued an undergraduate degree in a field of her choosing, she would not have any financial worries. I was willing and able to carry the burden of all financial responsibilities because I wanted her focus to be on school.

Initially, she told me that she wanted to attend a local university, but was not confident that she would be admitted into the program. I called and spoke to a few people in the office of admissions. I explained my sister's story and asked that she be given a chance. While I was not guaranteed that she would be admitted, I was advised that her application would be given serious consideration. Being the trusting brother and person that I am, I believed her when she told me she would apply to the university. As a result, I did not deem it necessary to continually check on her application status. I was in a state of bewilderment when I was advised by a university official that the application period was over and there was no application pending review for my sister. That is when the vicious cycle of deceit began.

I was not mad at her for long because we all have to walk our own path, and I understood that. My choices for an individual may not necessarily be his/her choices. I was confused as to why she would choose to work and pay bills when she had the option to work, study, pay no bills, and educate herself in the process. But, hey... who was I to question the intentions and the thought process of another grown human being? *Apparently nobody*, I thought. I was trying to set a good example for her and show her what life was really like outside of the hood, but she did not want to have any part of it. She had taken a job at the bank and was still working at the hair salon. She was busy and making her own money, but her thinking was extremely short-term. She did not understand that although she felt as if she was smooth sailing at that point, her lack of education was going to prove to be detrimental to her future. She was making life extremely difficult for herself and did not take the doctrine of unintended consequences seriously. She did not realize that she was putting herself at a distinct disadvantage by not taking advantage of any and all educational opportunities. She already had two strikes against her by being a young and black woman. Add uneducated to that mix, and what do you get? A virtually unemployable human—particularly in a tough economy.

I know it is bad to say, but that was her choice, and I tried to stop it. She taught me that no one can change another person unless that person wants to change.

The bank position was good for her, but her outside activities put her into contact with the wrong group of people. The same hood-type chicks that she so desperately wanted to get away from were the same type of girls that she became friends with while living in VA. I met some of her new friends and while they seemed nice and friendly, their motivations, ambitions, and intentions were quite transparent. I looked right through them. I told Stacy that those girls meant her more harm than good, but she would not listen. In her eyes, I was just being an overprotective brother. These girls were like wolves. They saw a new girl living in a new world without many friends and recognized that she could be easily influenced. They knew that she had an older brother who was trying to do right by her, but it would have made too much sense for them to tell her to follow my lead. Instead, they chose to walk her down a path of denial and deception.

I knew that her mind state was being compromised when she would make beyond ignorant statements. One of them was, "I live here just like you, and I can bring any boy over here that I want to bring." I occasionally heard, "You don't pay all of the bills around here, so you might as well shut the hell up talking to me." It angered me when she told me, "My friends make just as much money as you do, and they said I could live with one of them if I had to." There would be days when she would be away from home for fifteen to twenty consecutive hours and would not even attempt to call me and let me know that she was doing okay. I would call her cell phone, and she would not answer. I would call her friends' phones, and they would lie to me and say that she was not there. Her lack of appreciation and inability to focus were unreal. When she would talk crazy, I would calmly let her know that I understood her "friends" were hyping her up to say such nonsense, and I gave her the option to go and live with the girls who wanted to see her fail. I would explain to her that random boys did not have the option of running in and out of the crib at their leisure; and as long as I paid 95 percent of the bills, she had no control of that property.

It almost all came to a violent halt one afternoon before I went to class. One day, she came home mad about something and, being a concerned brother, I wanted to know if there was anything I could do to make the situation better. Complete loss of control and anarchy ensued. I am not sure what verbiage I used to send her over the edge, but she lost it and unleashed a tirade of insults and name calling that should have resulted in all of her front teeth being dislodged from her mouth. I asked her to lower her voice and to act as if she had some resemblance of sense. She slammed doors and acted like she owned the joint. As I tried to grab her hand to talk to her, she hit me like she had learned some new tricks in kickboxing class, or had just finished completing a fatality on *Mortal Kombat*. Reflexes caused me to grab her by the throat and throw her against a mirror. I had another out-of-body experience similar to when I encountered the situation with my dad as a senior in college. I held her up against the mirror with one hand while she was kicking, screaming, and holding on to what she probably thought were the last few seconds of her human existence. I was an alien to me at that point, and I know she was terrified. I am not sure how long I held her there, but it felt like an eternity. I released the grip that I had around her neck, and she was still crying uncontrollably.

The only thing I could do to calm myself down was to go to sleep. That was probably not the best thing to do since she could have killed me in my sleep, but she was terrified at that point and I was too mad to even consider other alternatives. That same evening, I sincerely apologized to her for putting my hands on her, and she apologized as well. Order in the universe was restored—at least for a few hours.

Some friends from work called me that night to go out. My school and work schedule usually forced me to say no, but as you can imagine, I needed to go out and have fun that night. I am glad I went, but I kind of wish that I would not have because the world as I knew it changed. Even though Lana and I had some difficulties in the past, there was no one else that I would have rather been with and called my girlfriend and/or future wife—until I met Marie. I drove to the predetermined location, got in the backseat of the car because I had no intention of driving, and was introduced to the new girl. She was sitting in the front seat, and I did not even look up to see what she looked like.

We get to our desired destination, and everyone got out and started walking. This was the point when curiosity set in. I saw that she had a nice build to her, had long hair, and had a different swag to her. She was the personification of confidence, and I was digging it. I was still cool, though, until we actually got in line to go into the nightclub. I tapped her on her shoulder in an effort to formally introduce myself and, more importantly, see what she looked like. When she turned around, I was lost. She was beautiful, to say the least. She had a perfect smile, stunning eyes, and a childlike innocence that grabbed me and would not let go. She had an immediate interest in me too, and I knew it. The chemistry was evident from the very beginning, and I think the entire group noticed it—kind of like a scene in a movie when a friend introduces his homeboy to a girl and when he looks up to greet her, he forgets his name. I had to remain cool, though. I could not let her and everyone around me in on my secret that I was at a loss for words and completely frazzled. The only words that went through my mind were "Uh-oh."

Once we were in the club, sparks began to turn into flames. It was as if we were the only two people in the room and the DJ was playing songs just for us. I had no interest in dancing with or talking to any other girls, and apparently she did not want to dance with or talk to another guy either because we were together almost the entire time. There was not a lot of conversation because it was too loud to actually talk and hear what the other person was saying. We would just look at each other and I would say to myself, *What is going on here?* Since I am not a mind reader, I am not sure what she was thinking, but I am sure it was similar to what I was thinking. On a couple of different occasions, the girls would come and take her away or the boys would come and get me, but it was never too long before we were right back dancing with each other again.

The night progressed and after we left the club, we got to a restaurant to hang out as a group. The attraction that we both shared was more than obvious at this point. People in the group were making jokes, but I did not care. Emotions were flying high. The only other girl that I had ever felt this way about was my current girlfriend, and we had been together for almost four years at this point. The night ended, and we all went our separate ways. I was sad though because even though I had not really done anything wrong, I felt like I had. I thought about Marie all night and could not wait to see her again the next day.

The next day was just as good as the prior night, except for the fact that we actually had to sit down and talk. I told her that I had a girlfriend, and she told me that she had a boyfriend. The timing of our encounter was all wrong. What made it worse was that we both felt that if the timing was different, we might have been a perfect match for each other. She loved sports as much as I did, she was working on a PhD, she was ambitious, she was feisty, and she loved talking s***. There was really nothing that could be done, though. I was in love with my girlfriend, and she was in love with her boyfriend. We hung out as much as possible for the remaining few days that she was in VA; and just as quickly as it began, it was over. I thought about her on a constant basis for quite some time, but I have not seen her since that weekend and have only talked to her via email a few times. Occasionally when I think about her I wonder if she is married. I do not know why we met that weekend or why we crossed paths, and even though nothing happened, it still makes for a good story.

Even though that weekend was good, Murphy's Law was still in full swing. It seemed as if there was no escape or end at sight. A few weeks went by, and I recognized that my sister was in a complete state of depression. She would sleep all day when she was not at work, was barely eating, and did not say more than ten words to me in a given day. I was able to self-manage my own emotions, but I was definitely not capable of managing the emotions of a young woman.

As I was driving home from working out one afternoon, I got a phone call from one of her friends. Initially, I thought she was calling to find out if I knew where my sister was, but that conversation changed tones very quickly. She proceeded to tell me that Stacy, Tiana's alter ego, had stolen a large sum of money from the salon. Her choice of words, vocal inflections, and pace of speech indicated to me that she was being honest. Stacy was in such a bad state of mind that she would have been willing to do anything to get attention. Her "friend" told me that the owner was about to call the police, press charges, and have her put in jail. Even though what she did was wrong, I could not allow that to happen. She was still my little sister, and family always comes first. I called the shop owner and asked him to please not call the police. I told him that I would have the money to him within forty-eight hours and promised him that it would never happen again. He agreed to my request, and I was more than thankful; I was furious.

As soon as I walked in the door at home, she knew something was wrong. I did not yell at her, or try to beat her senseless; I asked what possessed her to do something so distasteful and ignorant. As usual, the answer I was given was, "I don't know." This time, however, "I don't know" was not an acceptable answer.

I talked to her, expressed my disappointment, made her cry, and made her promise to do better. I gave her the money to repay the man and told her that the money needed to be back within forty-eight hours, or I was calling the police myself. She returned the money, apologized, and was told that her services at the salon were no longer needed. She was fortunate because that situation and the consequences could have been much worse.

Time continued on, and Stacy had not been involved in any more criminalistic endeavors. She still had her bank job, so everything was not lost in the fire. She was learning vast amounts of information as a result of working as a customer service representative. Her customer service skills were getting better, she was gaining an in-depth knowledge of how to handle money, and her communication skills were at an all-time high. Her self-confidence had increased. It seemed as if everything was going well… until she gave me a letter. When I read it, I was in a state of complete amazement and worry. I knew that she had to be dealing with a lot of things mentally, spiritually, and emotionally, but I did not fully understand the pain she was experiencing. She talked about how she felt as if she was letting the entire family down on an almost daily basis, how she was losing her faith in God and His teachings, and how she would often have serious suicidal thoughts. She explained how she did not feel as if she could succeed in this world and did not understand her purpose in life. How do you respond to something like that? I did not know. Did she want advice? Did she just want me to know how she felt? I had no idea. So I did what I felt was necessary. I sat her down and talked to her; well, I listened more than I talked because I felt that was what she wanted and needed. I was very worried for her because I felt that she was truly going to hurt herself or someone. The letter was written with a lot of thought and sincerity.

At this point, I knew she was not merely out to get attention. Something dangerous was bothering her, and she needed to tell someone. I was the closest one to her, maybe not emotionally, but in regards to proximity, so I was a viable option. She told me how she knew moving back to Flint might not necessarily be the best option, but that was where she was the most comfortable. I was not expecting that, and it made me mad actually. She was only paying about $700 per month, including her cell phone bill, to live in Northern Virginia, she had a good job at the bank, and she was gaining valuable life experiences. Moving back to Flint and returning to the hood life was the dumbest option she could have thought of was my take on the situation. Some not so educated people were talking her into making such an ignorant decision, and I knew it. She was a grown woman though, and there was nothing I could do other than tell her that I loved her and wished her luck. Disbelief and absolute amazement do not even accurately describe my feelings. The selfish side, or the devil in me, also began to take over my thoughts.

I began thinking I could not believe how selfish she was. I changed my entire life for her with no regard for my welfare and overall life plan. I felt that God wanted me to be there for her, so I knew that is what I had to do. I was beginning to think was it worth it? I withdrew several applications for graduate school, bought a $300,000 house for us to live in, and only made her pay $500 per month for rent. I decided not to go play basketball professionally in Portugal because I wanted to make sure her life was better; I kept her out of jail and, most importantly, gave her the opportunity to lead a better life. I was not being all self-righteous, but I thought that what I had done and was currently doing was the right thing because, in actuality, I did not have to do anything. I could have walked the path that I had originally chosen, but I chose otherwise.

A few weeks went by and she had not left, so I assumed she had changed her mind and was going to try to make the best out it. Wrong answer. As soon as I had that thought, she told me that our aunt was coming to get her. I was furious at that part of our family for assisting in such an unwise decision. They were supposed to motivate her to do better, not try to pull her back to mediocrity. I knew that Stacy was easily influenced and persuaded, but d***. I did not think she would allow such ignorance to take over her thought processes. I was sad and mad at the same time. I truly could not believe that family members would want to interfere with my sister's success. I had worked so hard to make a better life for her, and in the blink of an eye, their influence over her proved to be much stronger than mine.

The day that my aunt arrived was like a slap in the face to my family. Indirectly, her presence at my house told me that my willingness and ability to make a better life for my sister meant absolutely nothing and that with a few choice words, they could change the course of her thinking and, ultimately, her life. I thought she was going to leave on good terms, but as you have probably anticipated at this point, she did not. She had promised to pay me back the money I had given her to pay back the salon owner, she had promised to pay off her cell phone bill, and she also promised to pay of all miscellaneous bills that were incurred in the Northern Virginia area. None of that happened.

Either way, I was sad to see her go. I wanted her to be happy, but I felt like she was making the wrong decision. I felt like I had let her down in some way and that was why she was leaving. I know it was not at all about me, but that is how I felt. I did not want her to leave, but I could not do anything about it.

Just as quickly as my life had changed a year prior, it changed again. If you recall, my mortgage was $2100 per month, so the $500 she was giving to me every month was extremely helpful. All of sudden, it was gone. She never paid me back the money that I gave her to repay the salon owner, she left me with her $500 late cell phone bill payment, and she never cleared all of her other debts. Luckily, I had not cosigned anything for her so I did not receive any phone calls, only letters and "final notices" in the mail. I wrote off the money that she owed me as a loss, but what really ate me up on the inside is that she left without saying thank you. That hurt me, and it still bothers me. I changed my life for her, not once, but twice in the course of about sixteen months, and she did not even have the human decency to say, "Thanks, Jr., I appreciate what you did for me, and I am glad that you were there for me when I needed you the most." There was no appreciation and no gratitude. Apparently, I did something wrong because I thought the rules of engagement were different. I thought that if someone did something that Jesus would approve of, a mere thank you would be in order. But, hey, they crucified Him, so I guess I got off relatively easy.

Not all was lost, though, because during the same time she decided to leave, I was moved into an analytical and operational position at work, and that is exactly what I wanted, or so I thought. You know the old saying, "The grass is not always greener on the other side of the fence"? Well, it's true... it's not. As an analyst, I had the option of leaving right when I was supposed to leave so that I could go home, do homework, and prepare for class. Having the same analytical responsibilities and being involved in the preparation for operations was much more difficult than I had anticipated. I could no longer write a report and leave. I had to send it out for coordination and wait for responses. Much of the work was time sensitive, so I did not have the luxury to leave whenever I felt like it. In addition, I no longer had anyone to take care of Irish. So what did I do? I bought another dog—a $2100 Doberman pinscher, and I named him Kain.

Irish was sad after my sister left, so I had to do something to make him happy. For about three weeks after she left, he would just go into her room and sit. Sometimes he would jump on her bed and lay there for hours not even attempting to play with me or his toys. He had become extremely attached to her, and he had lost two friends in two years. First, Chase was taken away from him when EJ bought his first home, and now Tiana was gone. He needed another playmate, so I had to make things right in his world. Kain brought much enjoyment into both of our lives, but now I had doubled my responsibilities. I had to buy two of everything.

Once again, my life was in warp speed mode. I would wake up at 5:00 a.m. every morning, drive approximately an hour to work, work for about ten to twelve hours, drive an hour back home to feed and play with the dogs for a little bit, make sure my homework was done for that class, drive an hour to class, stay there for three hours, drive back home, do more homework, eat, and then attempt to sleep for three to four hours. That is a long sentence, so you know it was a long day. I tried not to complain because it was the life that I had chosen, and I knew it. I was in a privileged position so I had to remain vigilant in my efforts, and I had to persevere.

Work was good. Not only did I have more responsibilities, but my skill level was increasing rapidly and I was becoming very proficient at my daily activities. At the age of twenty-five, I was given high-level responsibilities. My analytical reports were seen by upper level government officials, and I also had the privilege of seeing how operations were planned and executed. My life experiences were getting better as the days went by, and I was becoming more savvy and creative in my new element. It was during this period when I met three of the most helpful and influential men I had ever met: Mac, Laz, and Joe.

Mac was very intelligent and perceptive. He always saw things as they could be and not as they were. He taught me how operations should be run, he taught me how to read between the lines of the analytical reports, he believed in me and always gave me hope and a sense that I could always do better. Becoming complacent was not an option as long as Mac was around. I tried so hard because I never wanted to let him down. I wanted to prove that his belief and faith in my abilities were not unwarranted.

Laz was a straight shooter and called things exactly as he saw them, good or bad. He was very encouraging and always told me to make myself a superstar. He never questioned my abilities and saw something in me that I still do not see in myself. I guess it was fatherly intuition.

Joe was like another big brother. He helped me become more of a gentleman; he talked to me about life, he talked to me about sports, and he gave me something to strive for. He was about ten years older than I was, and he seemed to have it all together. He was making a lot of money at work, had a beautiful wife and kids, and seemed to live every day as if it were his last. Every time I saw him, he was smiling or about to start smiling. Everything in his world seemed to be in place. Maybe that was not the case; but from the outside looking in, it sure seemed like it, and I wanted to emulate his actions.

I learned a lot of life lessons from those three men, and to them I say thank you. Their talks, phone calls, emails, and encouraging words meant more to me than I can even write in this book. If I had ten thousand tongues, I could not say thank you enough. So, Mac, Laz, and Joe, your efforts were not in vain. I am doing all right.

Tiana was gone and I was living at a frantic pace, but I was still living. I was doing well in school, the dogs were good, and it seemed as if the universe was conspiring to help me. I wanted to set an example for all young men from all walks of life that if you want to make it bad enough, you will. The fire that dwells deep inside every one of us only goes out if we put it out, or allow someone else to extinguish it. I wanted to be a living testament to people that the only limits placed on us are the limits we impose on ourselves. I thought of all the reasons why I could do things and never worried about or listened to those who gave me reasons why not. My focus was strong. It was sharp, and so was I. Everything in my world was good. It was moving fast, but it was good nonetheless. I could see the light at the end of the tunnel, but then the breakup happened.

THE BREAKUP

"I kind of thought that I would be better all by myself. I have never been so wrong before." Joss Stone sang these words in a song titled "Spoiled," and it is a pretty accurate description of how I felt about Lana. Two days before Valentine's Day, heartbreak ensued. I cried like a little baby who had lost his favorite blanket. I have often heard people say that it is better to have loved and lost than to not have loved at all. I am not entirely sure that I agree with that statement. To lose someone that, for all intents and purposes, taught me how to love was tough. The breakup was mutual, but I was entirely at fault. During our four-year relationship, I never opened up to her and told her how I really felt about things until that night; and by then, it was too late. Virtually every person in my life until I met her had figured out a way to walk away, and I put her in that box from the start. My thinking was, *I thought she was going to leave just like everyone else, so why give her a chance?* I did not talk about disappointments that I faced as a child, I did not talk about my fears and worries, and I did not talk about serious life issues. I kept her very close to me but only told her things that I wanted her to know. I never showed any signs of vulnerability because doing so, in my estimation, would have signified weakness. I was a closed vault, and she was never given the key.

For over four years, I would talk to Lana almost every night. I knew her life story, and she knew mine—well the things I told her, anyway. She would smile, laugh, and encourage me to try to do better. I did things with her that I never dreamed of doing. We would go to historical museums, art museums, watch chick flicks, and even hold hands sometimes. I know—crazy, right? She never pushed me, but I wanted to do better because I never wanted to disappoint her. Her path in life was not easier than mine, per se, just different. She always knew that she wanted to be a doctor, so her life outline was clear. I, on the other hand, had no idea and still really do not. Although I am a wanderer, I am never lost. There is a method behind the madness—organized chaos, if you will. There is nothing that I think I cannot do. There are some things I have decided that I do not want to do, but if necessary, I know that I could do them and excel. She would often try to get me to focus on a single path, but that is not what I wanted to do. I wanted to learn a lot about everything in an attempt to enhance my versatility and be considered a jack-of-all-trades. I wanted to figure out a way to add value to the world, and doing only one thing was not acceptable to me. After a while, I think she just gave up and figured I would find my way someday. Just to clarify, I am not saying that she gave up on me, just that she gave up on trying to focus my attentions in one particular direction.

Lana is beautiful, smart, fun, opinionated, determined, ambitious, churchgoing, and family-oriented. She was exactly what I needed at that point in my life and I think, well, I hope, I was the same for her. As a child, I was told that sometimes we meet people who come into our lives for a reason, some for a season, and some for a lifetime. I honestly thought that Lana was going to be in my life for a lifetime. While I think we will remain friends forever, it is not how I envisioned it while we were together. I thought we would be married, travel to several countries, and on the verge of having kids by now, but life does not always happen how we plan it. Again, I take absolute responsibility for that vision not coming true because God knows she tried. She would often plead with me to be more open with her, to show more affection, to talk to her about things that were bothering me, to allow her to help me get through the hard times, and to just let her love me how she wanted to love me. I did not because I could not. There were times that I really wanted to talk to her about an assortment of topics, but I literally could not do it. I was unable, mentally and emotionally, to open up to her.

In retrospect, I now realize that it was fear that crippled me and, ultimately, our relationship. The perpetual long distance did not help our cause, either. I often wonder what would have happened if we would have actually lived in the same city while we were together. In over four years, we never spent more than ten consecutive days together. Did the distance really make it worse? Hard to say, but it definitely did not help the situation. I vividly remember her repeatedly telling me that the distance was killing her, and she was not sure how long she could handle it. Hearing those statements always made me sad because there was little to nothing that I could do to change our current state of affairs. She was pursuing her dream of becoming a doctor, and I was just trying to figure things out. Basketball was over, and now I had to move on. My only problem was I was not quite sure how, or where to move.

The night of 12 February was a difficult time for me, and I am sure it was difficult for her as well. We both knew it was coming, and it was just a matter of when. Our lives were completely different at this point. She was doing her thing as a future doctor, and I was working for the government and in school trying to survive. We talked about life situations, and we were not on the same page. I wanted to have kids by the age of twenty-nine or thirty, and she wanted to wait until her mid-thirties. She is a professional woman and once she makes her decision on an issue, there is no changing it. Regardless of the fact that she is charming, persuasive, and a persistent individual, her stance is not likely to change. I loved it and I hated it all at the same time. She was unable to leave her location because of her commitment to medical school and residency, and I was not too keen on leaving my position to move there, because in my mind, there was nothing for me to do there. Many people have said that love conquers all and blah blah blah, but I had aspirations too, and I refused to move to a place where there were minimal, if any, opportunities, for me to do what I thought I wanted to do.

We were at a crossroads in our relationship, and there was no point in holding on. I loved her and she loved me, but we were doing each other a disservice. I could not physically be there for her on those lonely nights when she would come home from work or school mad at the world and needed someone to just give her a hug and say, "Everything will be okay." I could not, from my current location, look at her in the eyes and tell her that I loved her so that she truly believed me and knew that I meant every word that I said. I could only listen to her stories from afar. She needed someone better than me. Who am I to say what she needed? No one. All I know is that I did not want to hold her back from pursuing other options and being happy. If my being miserable, sad, and/or lonely would have allowed her to find happiness, then I was all for it. I could not handle seeing or hearing her cry. I told her in the beginning of our relationship that if I ever felt as if I was becoming the source of her pain, I would walk away from the situation. Her sadness, her tears, and her fears, I felt, were caused by me not being there with her. It was eating me up on the inside, and I did not like it. She meant the world to me. I prayed for her more than I prayed for myself, and I knew it was time to let go.

So that person who I thought was going to be with me for a lifetime was only there for a prolonged season. As my mom always says, "Life brings about a change. It may be easy and it may be hard, but one thing it will definitely be is a learning experience." A learning experience it was. She was the teacher, and I learned more from Lana than she will ever know.

Two days later, we had our final Valentine's Day dinner. It was fun, but it was not the same. There was a sense of sadness and unfulfilled desires in the air. I tried to make everything okay, but I do not think I did a good job. She flew back home the following day, and I began my journey as a single man. I thought it was going to be fun to date again and learn the life stories of others, but it was hard at first. My first few months of being single were tough. I did not approach girls to go on dates because I was afraid they might say no, or I might not know what to say since I had not been on the dating scene in quite some time.

In an effort to maintain my sanity, I kept myself busy. I worked longer hours, worked out harder, and I studied for longer periods of time. I figured if I stayed as busy as humanly possible, I would not have time to think about Lana and remember how stupid I was for letting her walk away. It was tough because I would still talk to her almost every day so it was kind of like we were still together, but not really. I wanted to know if she had started dating other guys; but then again, I really did not want to know. I wanted to know if she was happier with or without me, but I was afraid to ask the question because, what if she told me something that I did not want to hear? It seemed logical for us to just get back together and figure out a way to make it work, but I knew that was not going to happen. I thought that maybe in the future the stars would align and we would be together again, but at that particular moment in time, it was not meant to be. I did not know what to do. I was soul searching, trying to find answers to questions that I probably should not have even been asking.

So there I was in Virginia, alone, confused and full of questions. Was I born to lose, or was I being taught a lesson? I was not sure. All I knew was that I needed a change of scenery. I began looking for schools that would accept transfer credits since I was already twenty-one credits into my MBA program. I was especially looking for schools that were close to Lana so we could make our relationship work. I wanted to have the best of both worlds. I wanted her in my life, and I wanted to be enrolled in a nationally ranked and recognized graduate program. People often say you can't have your cake and eat it, too. Well, I do not subscribe to that school of thought. I believe that all you have to do is ask and you will receive. I began applying to nationally ranked business schools. I detailed my current situation to several admissions representatives and requested that transfer credits be accepted. Most schools were willing to grant me acceptance into their program since I had a 4.0 in my current MBA program, but they were not willing to accept transfer credits. I was not willing to start over, so certain universities were no longer an option for me.

I explained my plans and objectives to Lana, but she was not very supportive. Well, I take that back. She was not thrilled that I was not going to be able to move closer to her. I explained that I was very interested in the university, but was unwilling to start over since I had already earned twenty-one credits. I think she finally understood my point of view, but she still was not happy. Internally, I was a mess. I wanted us to be together, but I did not want my dreams and desires to take a backseat to anything.

It was a tough time for me; but one of my closest friends, Jahsir, helped me through much of it. He was there for me then and remains one of my closest friends to this day. We would talk, and he would always give me words of encouragement to aid in the decision-making process. We were good friends in college as well, but he was really a godsend during this time in my life. I solicited the advice of Jahsir and a few more confidants and was given the advice to apply to universities in the California system as well as the Texas system. I took their advice but also applied to Daniels College of Business in Denver. The California schools were unwilling to accept transfer credits, so they were no longer options. It came down to Daniels College of Business and the University of Texas at San Antonio. Both schools were nationally ranked and recognized, so either way I would have made a good decision. I decided that in order to make the best decision possible, it was necessary to visit both campuses and get a feel for the people, the towns, the classrooms, and the overall environment.

Denver was my first stop, and I immediately knew that I would not be happy there because it was too cold. I also did not get that "I can call this home" feeling on my visit. The faculty and staff were nice, the people were great, but it just was not for me. A few weeks later, I made a trip to San Antonio to visit the university and fell in love with the place. The MBA program was nationally ranked, the faculty and staff were all highly touted and distinguished in their particular areas of concentration, the weather was great, the girls were cute, the cost of living was much lower than Northern Virginia and, most importantly, they would accept transfer credits. It was a very easy decision for me, especially when I found out my friend, Ross, would be completing his pediatric dentist residency in San Antonio as well. God had opened a door for me, and I would have been foolish not to walk through it.

Life was starting to change, and my plans were beginning to manifest themselves. "Try not to get too excited, young man," was the answer from the universe. Lana said the worst five words I had ever heard in my twenty-five year existence, and I experienced the worst day of my life all in a two-week period. I explained to her that I was going to sell my home in Virginia and complete my MBA at the University of Texas at San Antonio.

After I finished sharing my excitement with her, she said, "I'm so disappointed in you."

I could not believe what I heard. Never in a million years would I have guessed that those words would have ever come out of her mouth. I was trying to make a better life for myself in the hopes that one day we could be together, and that was her response. *So what?* you are probably thinking. You are absolutely right. In the grand scheme of things, those words are not tragic; but the fact that they came from her saddened me. Any other sentence or combination of words would have rolled off my back, and I would not have given them a second thought. Unfortunately, she lost me with that comment. Here it is, several years later, and it still bothers me. "I'm so disappointed in you." No one had ever said anything even remotely close to that before. She may not have meant it this way, but what I heard is, "You are a failure." If I were to tell someone I was disappointed in him or her, I would essentially be saying that he or she failed me in some manner. I did not know what to say, so I stopped calling her for a while and tried to forget about her entirely.

To make matters worse, as I was in the preparation stage of studying for finals so that I could make the move to Texas and begin taking classes in the summer, I experienced, to date, the worst day of my life. I have not mentioned the name AJ so far in my story, but he was like a brother to me. We were so similar, yet we were so different. Our lives paralleled, but we were on different streets. AJ was a good kid. He was smart, eloquent, articulate, charming, outspoken, street savvy, and loyal—almost to a fault. He knew everything about me, and I knew everything about him. We had been in fights together, hollered at girls together, drank together, played sports together, laughed together, cried together, expressed our dreams, desires, and fears to one another. We were complete complements. God placed him in my life and me in his for a reason: to challenge each other and make each other strive for excellence and a better life than what we were currently experiencing. We always said to each other that we would see better days or die trying. We vowed to make a better life for ourselves and for our family members. Making it to the mountaintop was the goal. It was not a matter of if, but a matter of when.

AJ, I believe, had split personalities. He would get into a fight or do something beyond stupid; and after it was over, he acted as if nothing ever happened. The day before I moved to Virginia, he and I got into a fight with some cats who we saw hit one of our female friends. After the fight was over, he calmly, without a care in the world, looked at me and said, "I know the police are probably on their way, so how about we go get some food from Denny's before we go back to my house?" There was no concern for consequences, and he was an absolute free spirit.

I was, in essence, his filter and conscience. I would do my best to keep him out of trouble and make sure cooler heads prevailed when tragedy was the only other alternative. Many of the dudes who did not like him liked me, so I was able to prevent several negative altercations from occurring. After I moved away, that all changed. AJ and the love of his life, Kim, had broken up by then, so he did not have anyone to pull him away from darkness. Slowly but surely, he rejoined the thug life crusade; and his poor decision-making sent him to jail at the age of twenty-two.

I did not like the fact that he was caged up like an animal with little to no hope for rehabilitation. We would communicate through letters, but it was not the same. Life on the inside is not the same as life on the outside, or so I have been told. Our lives were polar opposites, but we remained close. I would tell him to keep his head to the sky and know that better days would come when he returned to "life outside of the walls."

He was released in December 2005 and was home by Christmas. I went to visit him at his home during the Christmas holidays, and his demeanor and disposition were ominous. His outlook on life was cynical, and his words would prove to be prophetic. I extended an offer for him to come live with me in Virginia. His response was, "Nah, cuz, I think I am just going to stick around here and spend time with family and friends because I don't think that I will be on this earth that much longer anyway." I brushed it off and described his words as "institutionalized ignorance." I told him that I was in complete disagreement with his thought process, and he needed to regain his positive outlook on life and everything that it had to offer. We switched the subject and never raised the issue again.

On 3 May 2006, I received a call from AJ. He explained that he had been trying to call me for about a week and did not understand why I had not called him back. I apologized, told him that I was studying for finals, and that I would see him the following week when I came home to celebrate my birthday and pending move from Virginia to Texas. I saw him the following week, but it was not for a birthday party; it was for his funeral.

On the night of 4 May 2006, my spiritual self was in a battle with evil forces, and I was losing. Before I go to bed every night, I say my prayers. I pray for myself and others, I ask for forgiveness, wisdom, discernment, understanding, and God's mercy. This is nothing unusual for me, as I have been doing it since a child. However, there was something different about this night. When I knelt to say my prayers, I could feel spirits of evil surrounding me. Every time I closed my eyes in an attempt to pray, it felt like something was hovering over me, and it was not an angel. I could not shake the feeling, and it was quite disturbing. I had studied for quite a while that day in preparation for my accounting final, which was on Saturday, 6 May, and initially I thought that anxiety was the cause. I quickly dismissed this thought because I was not thinking about numbers, definitions, or anything scholastic in nature. The forces were so strong that my dogs were barking as if something was in the house with us.

I tried to go to sleep at about 10:30 p.m. because I knew my alarm clock was going to ring at 5:13 a.m. I could not sleep, and I could not shake the feeling. I knew something was wrong, but I just did not know what. Even when I would begin to doze off to sleep, I could feel something grabbing me, holding me down, and trying to suffocate me. I was paralyzed with fear. I was asleep, but the dream was so vivid. Something was in my room, and I knew it. I could hear my dogs barking, but I could not say anything.

On 5 May 2006, at 3:47 a.m., I received the call, and the worst day of my life began. When I saw the name "Kim" pop up on my caller ID, I knew that it was not going to be a positive wake-up call. When I answered the phone I said to her, "Please don't tell me what I think you are about to tell me." What felt like an eternity passed and, in the midst of her tears and heartbreak, she uttered the words, "He's gone." She told me he had been shot three times and was dead. I did not believe her. I did not want to believe her. To hear someone tell you that someone you loved and treated like a brother was dead and you were not even there with him was heart-wrenching. The "If only I were there" theories came rushing through my head, and I was lost.

I hung up the phone and immediately called AJ's phone. The first time, there was no answer. I hung up and called again. This time, another childhood friend of AJ's answered, and I knew it was true.

I said to him, "Put AJ on the phone."

He told me that he couldn't.

"I need to talk to AJ. Give him the f****** phone" was my response.

He quietly told me that AJ had been shot and was undergoing emergency surgery. At that time he was not dead, and I was going to hold on to even the smallest thread of hope. The only thing I could do was to ask God to not take my brother away from me. I called Moms and cried like a baby. I told her AJ had been shot and that the outcome of the surgery was unknown. As usual, she spoke calming words, and I believed that he was going to make it through. I regained my composure, got dressed, and went to work. I really do not remember the time, but sometime between 8:00 a.m. and 10:30 a.m., Kim called me again and told me that it was official. God had called him home. My brother from another mother had checked out of the game. The one person, other than my mom, that I always thought was going to be with me forever was gone.

I cried like a small child. I could not help it. I cried so much that I could not cry anymore. Coworkers tried to make me feel better, but it did not work. I made it through most of the day but had to leave early. By the time I arrived at my house, I was blinded by inconsumable rage, and the idea of taking the killer's life seemed reasonable. The only thing I could think about doing was finding the person who killed AJ and dissecting him like a lab rat. Mentally, I had committed one of the seven deadly sins: wrath. I had lost all regard for human life and wanted nothing more than to put several bullets into the body of the murdering son of a b**** who killed my brother. I know that I was not the only person who felt this way because although AJ had many enemies, he had just as many, if not more, friends. The only thing that really stopped me from going on a manhunt was the fact that I was about 600 miles away from home. In actuality, there was nothing that I could do about it. I did hope, however, that someone from Flint would find the kid who pulled the trigger and kill him on the spot.

I knew it was more than terrible to wish death upon anyone; but at that moment in time, I was not in a good frame of mind. I prayed and prayed and prayed some more. I asked God to please take such demonic thoughts away from me and help me through this time. I prayed for his family, his friends, and everyone that he came into contact with. I took my accounting test the next day, and it was like a dream. I tried to focus and although I was not there at the time of the shooting, I kept seeing the bullets hit his body until he was no longer breathing. Mentally, spiritually, and emotionally, I was in a state of complete darkness. I was in no shape to take any type of test, but I did it anyway. I still have no idea how I did on that test because in the grand scheme of things, it really did not matter. I just wanted to get home to see my brother before he was taken to his final resting place.

I arrived home on 11 May 2006, the day before my twenty-sixth birthday and the day before AJ was to be buried. There was a celebration of life and a celebration of death all on the same day. I guess I could have looked at his death as a celebration of life as well since I knew he was in heaven dancing with the angels and watching over us, but I didn't. That birthday sucked and to see a loved one in a casket was the worst birthday gift imaginable. To add insult to injury, it was pouring rain outside. Maybe the universe was crying because one of its earthly angels was no longer on earth. How can you live as an angel when you live in hell on earth? You can't, and none of us are angels, but I still like to believe that he was trying. AJ was a friend, a brother, a son, a future father, and a comet in a planet full of stars. He was sent to us to shine brightly and then fizzle away, but not before making a major impact in the lives of everyone he encountered. He had the heart of a king and a soul of a disciple. When he was taken to the burial site, a part of me went with him. I was unable to go to the gravesite because that would have made it too final for me. In fact, almost six years have passed and I still have not been, and I still have his phone number programmed into my phone. That might seem crazy, but I bet I am not the only one. I have grown stronger spiritually, mentally, and emotionally over the past six years, and the next time I go home, I will visit him. I am ready now... I think.

The day he was buried, 12 May 2006, I stopped living solely for me and began living for him as well. There were so many things that I wished I could have told AJ before he was taken away from us, and not doing so taught me a valuable life lesson. I learned that when you love someone or have something to say to someone, it is your obligation to do so because that person may not be around for as long as you think, and everything you wanted to say to that individual will be forever lost.

R. Kelly wrote a song that describes, almost perfectly, the things I wish I would have said, but never had the chance to. In an effort to maintain some level of censorship, I will replace the "N" word with the word *brotha*. The words are as follows:

> Brotha, we have been through a whole lot of things together, from running these streets to being down for whatever. And now that you gone, I gotta whole lot of

stuff to tell ya—things I should have said way back when we were younger.

There is a lot more to this song, but those couple of lines do an excellent job of summing up at least a little bit of what I felt and still feel. Man, I miss him. I know he is in a better place though, but it is still hard. Not a day goes by where something doesn't remind me of him. I know there are many people out there who have endured similar situations, and it is important for them to know that they are not alone. Other people feel their pain; and although their loved one or loved ones may not be with them in physical form, in their hearts, they will remain forever.

After AJ died, I really did not have anyone to talk to and really listen to me. I did not want anyone to talk to or listen to me for so long and when I decided I was ready, there was no one there to answer the call. I was all alone in a world that preys on the weak. However, I would not falter. I would show no external signs of weakness, and I decided to answer my own call. I learned how to listen to the whispers so that I would no longer have to hear the screams. I began looking for answers and no longer wanted to hear echoes.

Lana was no longer there for me and, as I previously mentioned, that was my fault. At this point in her life, she was so consumed with medical school that my sob stories were of no consequence to her. I would talk to her on the phone and she would say she was listening, but I felt otherwise. She felt it was her obligation to say things such as, "Aww, I'm sorry to hear that," or "Are you okay?" or "It will get better, trust me." Immediately after hearing my nonsense stories, she would begin a story about medical school and how hard her life was. I would listen but knew that she was lost in thought, and I was no longer a significant portion of her world. Anyone who has experienced such a love and lost it understands my sentiments. Maybe it was a self-fulfilling prophecy, but as I had anticipated four years prior, she walked away from me also—maybe not intentionally, but the result was the same.

AJ was gone, Lana was gone, and I was six hundred miles away from family and working too many hours to develop any other meaningful relationships. Irish and Kain were the only air-breathing mammals in my world that were there for me. Mom was always there, but she was in Michigan. The dogs, no matter what, always made me smile. I was lost, confused, hurt, sad, angry, and yet determined to make things better.

I was glad I was moving to Texas because I needed a change of scenery. I wish my brother could have been with me as I began another journey in my life, but unfortunately, he was not. Before I left, he did make his presence known one more time. On my last day of work, before the movers came to get my stuff, the day began as normal. I woke up at 5:13 a.m., got dressed, let the dogs out, ate breakfast, turned off all of the lights in the house except the light over the dog crates, and left home for work. The workday was good; I said my good-byes, expressed my appreciation and gratitude to all of those who helped me along the way, and promised to do my best in this world. They all wished me luck, and I was on my way.

When I returned home, nothing was the way I left it. Remember, the only light I ever left on was the light in the basement above the dog crates. When I opened the door, I felt like something or someone was in the house, but I was not scared. Every light was turned on, almost every cabinet door was open, all bathroom doors were open, and my CD player was playing Tupac's "Life Goes On": "How many brothas fell victim to the street, rest in peace young playa, there's a heaven for a G. I would be a lie if I told you that I never thought of death, my brotha, we the last ones left." Those were the words that were playing as I stood in my living room crying. I knew AJ had come home to check on me and felt it necessary to play on joke on me by turning on every light, opening every door, and turning on Pac's song. The dogs were as calm as could be, so I knew there was nothing wrong. I just smiled and said, "I miss you, man, and I will make it happen, one way or another." At that point, I already had the "Heart of a King, Soul of a Disciple," along with AJ's name and his date of birth/date of death tattooed on the insides of my arms. He is forever in my heart and will remain there until my dying day.

Early the next morning, the movers took my stuff away, and I was off to a new adventure. I was headed to the Lone Star state. I thought life was going to be much easier, but who was I kidding? Easy would not have made it fun. Externally I looked like I had it all under control. Internally, however, a downward spiral had begun. I was on my way to a seething hot bed of iniquity and vice in which a web of deceit and treachery would lead me to do things that I never would have imagined.

DOWNWARD SPIRAL

My travels to San Antonio should have been an indication that my Texas adventure was going to be more than interesting. About ten hours into my journey, I received a phone call from my Realtor in San Antonio saying that the deal on the house might not go through because the house did not appraise for the appropriate value. I was advised to call the lending company in order to figure out a way to get the necessary financing so that the scheduled closing would be successful. I called the Realtor in San Antonio and told her to advise the sellers that I was having minor difficulties with the lender, but not to worry because it would all work out the way it was supposed to. I had to believe that; I really did not have a choice. The drive to San Antonio took about two days, and I was on the phone with representatives from the lending company for a vast majority of that time. I dealt with some of the most unprofessional and incompetent human beings on the planet. There was a complete lack of customer service and concern for the welfare of their client. I spoke to approximately ten different people and got ten different answers on how to solve the same problem. There was no cohesion to the group, there was a complete lack of communication between the managers and line employees, and no one seemed to know what to do. I guess that is why they were experiencing such financial difficulties in 2008.

I arrived in San Antonio and had no place to go other than the Marriott Residence Inn. Although it was quite expensive, it was the only place that would allow me to house Irish and Kain. I was there for six nights trying to figure everything out.

When I arrived at the hotel, I called the moving company and asked them to delay my shipment and deliver my personal items last. Fortunately, they granted my request and told me that they would deliver my items in one week. Excellent, at least I had a week to figure it all out.

When I was in the sixth grade, my teacher, Mr. W, said, "Instead of crying when life throws you a curve ball, reposition yourself and smack it out of the ballpark as well." That is exactly what I had to do during my first week in Texas. A preacher once told me that whenever I felt as if I was in some type of crisis or found myself in an unwanted situation to ask myself, "In five years, will this matter?" In retrospect, most of the time the answer is no, but while you are in it, the situation seems so much worse.

The representatives did not have an answer for me and stopped returning my phone calls and emails. I was in a bad position. My home in Virginia had not sold, my furniture was on its way to Texas, the sellers of the Texas home were losing confidence in the deal, and I had lost all confidence in the lending institution. In an effort to make my life easier, I cut my losses and terminated my relationship with that organization. I had four days to find another lender, get them to close the deal, and move into my new home. All I could do was pray and ask that God figure out a way to make it work. Classes were starting on Monday, and I wanted to be in my house by then.

My Realtor put me into contact with a local lender, and everything seemed to fall in place. The house appraised, I was quoted a decent interest rate, the sellers gained an increased level of confidence, and I was going to be able to move into the home. The lender expedited the closing process, and we were guaranteed a closing date within fifteen days. The sellers agreed that I could move into the home as scheduled even though the actual closing would not take place for another fifteen days. I was ecstatic because the movers could actually bring my personal effects to the home instead of putting them into storage, and I would be able to sleep in my bed before grad school began. The house was lovely: 2500-plus square feet, a huge backyard for the dogs, an island kitchen, three bathrooms, three bedrooms, and a study room. Two weeks later, the closing process occurred and the home was officially mine. At the age of twenty-six, I had purchased my second home—not bad for someone who statistics said would no longer be living by that age.

As I was driving home after the closing was officially over, my Realtor in Virginia called me and told me that a buyer had put a contract on my home. I was overjoyed and extremely thankful. I did not know how I was going to pay two mortgages, but people always say that "God might not come when you call, but He is always on time." The housing market had begun its downturn just as I put my house on the market, and it was much more difficult to sell than I anticipated. Two months prior, my neighbor put his house on the market, and he had an overwhelming response rate. On the third day, he had seventeen contract proposals and accepted an agreement that would give him $30K more than his asking price and an overall profit of $80K. I was hoping that I would have the same fortune, but that was not the case. My home sat on the market for about two months before an actual deal was structured. I did not receive an overall profit of $80K due to the sale of my home, but I was able to pay off all credit card bills, finance my move from Virginia to Texas, and send Moms a little money. There was no spending money left, but at least I was blessed enough to take care of the important things. Mentally, I was in a better state knowing that I would not have to pay two mortgages. I knew that I would not work full-time while in school, so I took out a $40K student loan to help pay for school, living expenses, and miscellaneous things. Doing well in my MBA program was my number-one priority, and I did not want to have any major financial concerns while in school.

The University of Texas at San Antonio was very good to me. With the help of some contacts from Notre Dame, I walked into a sports marketing internship and had the opportunity to learn from two of the coolest people I ever met: Kirk and Quincy. Both men were about three years older than me, already had their master's degrees, and were doing well in their chosen career field. Quincy was more of the analytical type, and Kirk was the "pull-the-trigger" and get-it-done type of guy. I loved his style because he would make decisions and ask questions after the fact. They were both very forward thinking, and I learned a lot from them both.

During my first week, as I was being introduced to other staff members and some of the student athletes, I was given a warning by Kirk and a senior administrator on staff to be careful of all the girls running around. Many people, particularly the girls, got "new guy syndrome." I was not that much older than some of the student athletes, I was black, and questions were being asked about who I was, why was I there, and how did I get there. I loved that my life was a mystery to them. I was back on a college campus, and the fact that I blended right in was a blessing and a curse. I did not want to go back into hunter mode, but I did not have a real reason not to. My brother was in heaven, Lana was only in the picture from the periphery, I felt lonely, and social experimentation did not seem like such a bad idea. I was also advised that since I was really only a grad student and not on a payroll within the athletics department, it was okay for me to be a kid again. I had just left the work world, and I knew that those advisors were absolutely right. Once school was over and I re-entered corporate America, I knew that I would no longer be able to say and/or do anything without fear of consequences. That shark-like mentality allowed me to swim fearlessly into uncharted waters. Was it good? Maybe. Was it bad? I don't know. What I do know is there are many memories and many learning experiences and life lessons learned during my time in the Lone Star state. On the outside, life was good; but about a month after landing in San Antonio, I began a downward spiral that almost led to my death. Let's start from the beginning.

As usual, school was not a major concern of mine. I knew I would do well. My goal was to leave my MBA program with a 4.0. There was nothing in me that told me that I was not intelligent enough to make it happen, so I figured since I was back in school I might as well get all A's. I wanted to be recognized as one of the top MBA students to ever go through the program. The world taught me that if I did well in school, and had a genuine concern for the welfare and positive advancement of others, I would be rewarded in the future. School was school and I had a genuine concern for others, so everything should have worked out fine. I just had to do my part. I definitely started off on the right track.

About a month into my program, I was in full stride. Although I still talked to Lana on a semi-regular basis, she was not really in the picture and, to make matters worse, AJ was dead. I had lost all regard for human feelings and just wanted to do well in school and have as much fun as possible. I would ask girls out just because I did not have anything better to do. I had no intention of keeping them around for long. Get in, get out—the OG classic. It all started out innocently. It was all a game to me. I did not want to hurt anyone's feelings, and I was definitely in no position to have my feelings hurt.

First, it was a girl from the pet store. She had tattoos, I had tattoos, so I figured let's play. While dating her, an athlete began her pursuit. Now, we all know it is quite common for a single male to date more than one girl at a time and vice versa. So within the first month, my roster was beginning to increase. I was having fun. There was no real commitment to anyone, and all I really had to do was focus on excelling in the classroom and in the work environment. If time permitted and they wanted to hang out, I would. If I was too busy or if she was too busy, we wouldn't. Guys and women oftentimes talk about having friends with benefits.

Well let me tell you, no one does it well, and women do it even worse. They tell you that they do not want to have a relationship and that they want to have no-strings-attached fun just like you, but that story changes quicker than you think. This is not me telling you something I have heard or read about in a book; my words are due to personal life experiences. I have had that "Well, I thought you didn't want to have a relationship" conversation on more occasions than I would like to remember. Those two experiments lasted for a few months and just as quickly as they started, they were over. It was all good, though; I met a couple of new friends and had quite a bit of fun in the process. My first flight with Texas girls on board, and I had a smooth takeoff and a smooth landing.

Aside from going to school, working out, and dating random girls, I wanted to do something more constructive with my free time, so I decided to participate in a community outreach program. I made the phone call and inquired about what was necessary to be involved in such a program. I was advised to attend an orientation program in which all of the details would be outlined. I attended the orientation and on that day, the downward spiral began. As I sat in the classroom listening to the history of the program and how important it was to give back to the community, a woman emerged from the back room, and my focus switched to her. I tried not to make it obvious and still somewhat listen to the presentation, but it had become a little more difficult to do so. She stood about 5'10," had long brownish hair, and was built beautifully. The only problem was she had on a wedding ring. That fact alone meant that she was off-limits.

After the orientation was over, all of the volunteers and staff members were officially introduced to each other and when I met her, I did my best to shorten the small talk and figure out a way to get out of there. Up until that point in my life, I had not interacted with a married woman that was near my age. While living in Virginia, a friend told me that he had a slip up before and advised how aggressive married women could be. When he told me the story, I assumed his level of will power was limited and he did not have any self-restraint. That could not have been further from the truth. He was a very strong-willed cat, but when something like that is handed to you, with no strings attached, it is very difficult to say how you will react. I ended the pleasantries and left the building.

As I walked into my house to get ready for work, my cell phone rang. I usually do not answer phone numbers that are not programmed into my phone, but I recognized this number as being from the volunteer organization. I answer the phone and, lo and behold, it was Kai on the other end. She began to tell me that she knew that I was new in the area like she was and wanted to let me know that if I ever needed any assistance from anyone at the volunteer organization to let her know. That was nice of her, and I appreciated her sincerity. She then went on to ask me if I had one of the famed Internet communication tools, i.e., Yahoo! Messenger, AOL Instant Messenger, MySpace, Facebook, etc. I told her that I did, and she laughed and told me that she had already found me on one of those sites. Again, I did not think anything of it because I used MySpace or Facebook to look up friends or people I had recently met all the time, so her telling me that was nothing out of the ordinary.

She proceeded to say, "Now this might sound a little strange, but my husband is going to be out of town this weekend, and I was wondering if you would like to hang out with me and some of the people I have met since I have been in town." She explained that she would be meeting up with other volunteers, some people from the gym, and others through mutual friend introductions. I did not want to go but figured why not. A bunch of people were going, so it should be a fun night. She asked me if I would come and pick her and a couple of her single friends up from her house because they were going to be drinking and did not want to drive.

"Uhhh, I guess so" was my answer. She gave me her address, and I told her that I would call her later that evening once I got home from class and finished a little homework. I was a little nervous, but not really, because she and I were not going to be alone. In addition, I considered myself to be a strong-willed person and as having the ability to say no if necessary.

The day went by and I got more excited at the thought of meeting some new single girls. I did not necessarily want a girlfriend at that point, but I did want female companionship. I finished class, knocked out some homework, and texted Kai. She told me that they were getting dressed and would be ready to go once I got there. As I look back on it, I know I was trippin' that night because I drove about forty minutes in the total opposite direction of where the bar was just to pick some girls up.

Anyway, I got to her house, and she invited me in. She lived in a lovely house. It was about 3000 square feet, immaculate, and professionally decorated. There were pictures all over the house of her and her husband. *What a happy couple,* I thought. She gave me the tour of the home and introduced me to her friend. She explained that the rest of the people were going to meet us at the bar, but she wanted her best friend to ride with us. Her friend was very cute, so I was under the impression that she had brought her for me. I was single and her friend was single, so it at least made sense. Wrong impression. Her friend was there as a decoy.

As we were driving to the club, I find out that her friend had a boyfriend as well. That was clue number one. As we were walking down the street to the club, a guy handed me a card. On one side it read, "Jabez cried out to the God of Israel, 'Oh, that you would bless me and enlarge my territory! Let your hand be with me, and keep me from harm so that I will be free from pain.' And God granted his request—1 Chronicles 4:10." On the other side it read, "Do not fear, for I am with you; do not be dismayed, for I am your God. I will strengthen you and help you; I will uphold you with my righteous right hand—Isaiah 41: 10." How insightful. Clue number two.

After having a few drinks, Kai decided she wanted to dance with me. I like to have fun and dance as well, so her request was immediately granted. As we danced, I could feel her getting closer and closer and wanting to do more than just dance. She told me that she had never done anything like this before, but for whatever reasons, she could not help herself and wanted to do any and everything sexual with me. My initial response to that was no. I was flattered by the offer, but I knew she was married and I did not want to get mixed up in some kind of homicidal drama. As the night progressed, she became even more aggressive and candid in her speech. Her friend even began talking to me on her behalf. She would say things like, "My girl is fa' real feeling you," "You should fa' real take care of that," "Fa' real, C, you need to give her what she wants." She was very amusing to me because she said "fa' real" about 7000 times that night.

I was able to respectfully decline the advances while we were at the bar, but I knew it was going to be tougher once I got back to her house. I dropped her friend off at her car and in prophetic fashion, or maybe it was self-fulfilling prophecy, my concerns became real. She began her attack, and I was like a lost, little boy. My efforts to say no were almost futile, and some of her advances were accepted. She asked me to sleep with her in her bed; but at that point, I was not completely on the dark side, and an adamant "absolutely not" was my answer. There was no way in h*** that I was going to have sex with her in their house and definitely not in their bedroom and in their bed. In my mind, that was not even an option.

After about an hour of failed persuasion techniques on her part, I decided I had to go home. My body was saying stay, but my mind was saying no. My mind was victorious that night. I left Kai's home. As I was driving, the text messaging started. She told me that she wanted to see me again as soon as possible, that she wanted to strip for me, that she wanted me to be her break from reality, and that there would be absolutely no strings attached. I think the "no strings attached" part is what really caught my attention. I mentioned earlier that no one does that well, and girls do it even worse. Well, this time it was different. She was married and could not get mad if she saw me out with someone else or if I did not have time to hang out or whatever. To me, that was a pretty enticing deal. I told her that I would never step foot into her house again, but she was more than welcome to come and visit me. She decided that she wanted to come over to my place and have a Blockbuster night the following night. I agreed.

The night began innocently enough. We talked, had a few drinks, and began to watch the *Lion King*. A few drinks turned into more drinks, and more drinks led to a loss of all inhibitions. The downward spiral had officially begun. I felt terrible after the fact. I know sin is sin either way you look at it, and one isn't worse than the other, but being involved in an adulterous act seemed to be so much worse. It was like I blatantly ignored one of the Ten Commandments and made God mad on purpose. I immediately tried to justify my actions and project the blame. I tried to tell myself that I was not married, so technically I did not do anything wrong.

I called EJ and Jones because I needed someone to talk to. I did not want to brag about the situation, but I did not want to keep it bottled up inside of me. EJ was quite understanding of my situation. He also told me that it was going to be hard to stop, especially because there were no strings attached. I believed him because he seemed to speak from experience. I told Jones that I refused to do anything with her at her house out of respect for her husband. He laughed and said, "What difference does it make? Do you think her husband would be more forgiving if he found out that you took her back to your house to do it as opposed to his? I think not. So all you did was waste gas."

He was right, and all we could do was laugh. It was fun, though. I figured that I wouldn't do it again, but I was completely wrong. My mind said stop, but the body was in complete control. Many people say that if you cross a line once, it becomes easier and easier to cross that line. Once that line has been crossed too many times, it disappears and what once seemed wrong is actually perceived as being normal. If I would not have experienced such personal character degradation, I would not believe it, either. Trust me, though; it is true. I am not sure what her husband did to make her skate on him like that, but whatever it was, she did not like it. She was a master in the art of deception, and I was right there with her.

The next five months were like a whirlwind, and I was officially fighting an internal battle. Kai came over to "Fantasy Island" almost every weekend—sometimes during the week for her lunch break, and sometimes before I went to class. For five consecutive months, this went on, and I drank to the point of intoxication virtually every weekend. There were even times when I would go to class drunk. I really did not handle the breakup with Lana and AJ's death well at all. No one ever knew, though. I was doing extremely well in the academic environment, and I was the "go-to" graduate student in the sports marketing department. I was functional but at the same time developing alcoholic tendencies. I could take five to seven shots of Patron and immediately thereafter write a coherent and intelligible paper to be reviewed by a professor.

At this point in my life, I would have at least three shots of tequila or vodka four to five nights per week. I was fighting a battle with myself, and I was losing. I tried to talk to a couple of friends about it, but no one really understood. All of my homeboys thought it was admirable to engage in such devious acts and thought there was nothing better than having a no-strings-attached relationship with an older woman. While that may have been true, I needed someone to help me figure out how to stop it and not encourage the behavior. Kai was a queen seductress. Every time I would try to pull away, she would figure out a way to bring me right back. I do not blame her for my activities, though. It was a personal choice to indulge in such sinful pleasures, and I have always accepted full responsibility for my actions.

I thought the vicious cycle was going to end when I met Teresa at a basketball game. She had such a childlike innocence and vibrant personality that I was immediately drawn to her. I thought that if I could find someone to occupy my mind and time, I would be able to escape the voluntary and habitual act of stealing another man's wife. Teresa was fun, smart, beautiful, ambitious, and strong-willed. She single-handedly restored my faith in the decency and good will of human beings. Our relationship should have turned into a lot more than it did, but again, I blame myself for messing up the potential for something good. I was in a bad frame of mind and, although I knew that I liked her, escaping the almost cult-like power that Kai had over me was going to be extremely difficult. Like most men, I started off doing all of the little things. I would send her text messages in the morning to let her know that I was thinking about her, I would visit her often, I would dog-sit for her, I would study with her, and I would send her gifts that said, "I'm thinking about you." I tried not to lose interest; and to be fair to her, I don't think I did. I do, however, think that I veered off the path of straight and narrow because of my mind-set.

At this point in the story, I did want a girlfriend. I wanted to have someone around who was supportive of my ideas, goals, and aspirations. I felt like there was a void in my life, but I couldn't quite figure out what it was. Lana was always in the back of my mind, but I refused to let my past dictate my future; I knew it was there to simply serve as a reminder of what I had been through and a guide to help me bridge the gap from where I was to where I wanted to be. I did my best to be the guy that I knew I once was. I was in a self-transformative mode and desired the participation of another in my evolutionary journey. Consequently, I decided that I was going to stop drinking five nights per week, deal with only one girl, and refocus myself on the things in my life that mattered the most: God, my family, and my friends. In order to accomplish such an objective, I knew that I was going to have to remove Kai from the picture. I really did not have many opportunities to talk to her other than when we were engaged in playing the "grown people game," so I wrote her the following letter:

> I want you to know that I am writing you this letter because I know it will be easier for me to say everything that needs to be said and easier for you to read instead of hearing me say it. First of all, I want to apologize for my part in the things that have been done. I really enjoy the time we have spent together, but in an effort to save our souls, I think it has to stop. After the last time you came over, I had one of the most vivid dreams in my life...one of those that seemed too real. Anyway, I know I was asleep, but it felt like I was awake and all I could hear was a voice saying you have to stop doing what you are doing because you know it is wrong. I feel that neither one of us will get blessed to our full potential if we keep blatantly ignoring the rules. I know that it is fun and a break from reality, but I do not want anything to go wrong. Your personal life is very important and I do not want to be the cause of that going bad. I feel terribly about it already. You are a wonderful young woman and we probably should not have started playing the game from the beginning. Oh well, nothing we can do about that now, but we can stop it from happening again. Although my body does not want to (trust me, it doesn't), my heart and soul are telling me that it is the right thing to do. When we are together it is like a fantasy world that can only last for a short period of time because I know when you leave, we both have to go back to reality. Right now, we can separate the two, but I am afraid that if it continues it will start to get much harder to differentiate fantasy from reality...and that is when the real and

dangerous problems will begin. So to prevent that from even remotely occurring, we should lay back and just chill on it. I hope you agree. The crazy part about it is, the decision really has nothing to do with me or you while we are on this earth, but it has everything to do with us in regards to the afterlife. I have asked God to forgive me and I know he has... I am also asking that you forgive me as well for my part in it. I believe that God has a calling on all of our lives and he will not continue to bless us and keep us in his Divine favor if we continue to purposely do the wrong things. I, well we, cannot continue doing wrong and then ask God for forgiveness because it won't be sincere and my concern is one day the forgiveness will stop. As I said earlier, in an effort to save our souls, receive all the blessings that God has planned for us, and live long lives in which we prosper and make a difference in the lives of others, we have to stop.

You have no idea how hard it was for me to sit down and write this. I am giving away a no strings attached, free roller coaster ride—Oh well. I could write more, but for the sake of time I will end it here. I hope you understand and agree with everything that I have said. I hadn't really even thought anything about it until that dream... it was like an Angel or some supernatural power was really talking to me saying talk to her and let her know that it has to come to an end whether you two want it to or not. Even though it is fun and a break from our routine daily lives, it has never been, is not, and will not ever be the right thing to do. We do still need to be friends though... Can that happen without me being the wolf and you being the sheep? ;) Holla back at me... Let me know what you think.

She did not write back, but the next time I saw her, she told me that she agreed and appreciated my honesty. We accepted the idea of just being friends and began the journey to go our separate ways. I was free. I asked for forgiveness and by the grace of God, I knew that it had been bestowed upon me.

I was now able to give my undivided attention to Teresa, and she had it for about seven/eight months. Unfortunately, she just happened to meet me at the wrong time. About the seven/eight-month mark, I began planning my next move. I had to figure out if I was going to stay in my current location, or find employment in another state. I had a feeling that Texas was not going to be my final stop, so I began to distance myself from Teresa for her sake. She really liked me, and I liked her. As a result, I did not want to just walk away from her without any justifiable reasons. I did not want to be the source of another girl's pain, so I figured I would just project blame onto situational circumstances. I knew my actions were going to break her heart, but I thought that I was doing the right thing. I did not want her to continue down a path that led to a dead end. I knew that I was going to leave, and I knew that she was not going to be able to come with me. She was still in school, and her leaving all that behind for a boy was not even an option.

How did I distance myself? I stopped doing the little things. The early morning text messages stopped, the midday lunch visits ceased, the together time spent during study sessions declined, and I virtually became a closed vault...again. I did not talk to her about future plans, and I simply told her that I knew I was going to leave soon. Even though I cared about her feelings, I understood I needed to separate from her even if I couldn't put my finger on why. Anyway, I went to her house, told her my situation and, as I anticipated, she was heartbroken and in tears. All I could do was hold her and apologize. Sadness turned to anger and that same night, she played the "grown people game" with someone else. I found out through a friend a couple of days later, and when I asked her about it, she hesitantly told me that it was true. I wasn't devastated, but I was hurt by it. Her actions and her admitting to those actions presented me with the opportunity to walk away for good, and that is what I did. She would come by every now and then and we would have fun, but all emotions were gone. I was back where I started.

At this point, I did not have to worry about any girls on a serious emotional level. I had female friends that I would go and chill with, but I was not attached to anyone. Kai was out of the picture, Teresa was doing her thing, and I was able to focus 100 percent on me. I was doing very well in my MBA program, 4.0 at the time, and decided that I wanted to participate in a study abroad program known as the North American Summer School of Advanced Management (NASSAM). It was a tri-lateral program, and students from the U.S., Canada, and Mexico were invited to attend. Our class was relatively small: four Americans, four Mexicans, and four Canadians. The program was extremely intense. We participated in negotiation simulations, heard lectures from top-level business people all over the world, wrote a viable business plan, and had the opportunity to present the plans to venture capitalists in order to assess the feasibility of the plans.

We had a phenomenal group. Being immersed in different cultures and hearing about the lifestyles of other people is an extremely rewarding experience, one in which I think everyone should have the opportunity to enjoy if at all possible. I was able to make many contacts while in the program, and I had high hopes that finding a job upon graduation was going to be an easy task. My grades were exceptional, I had many high-level contacts within several industries, and I was involved in many extracurricular activities. There was no doubt in my mind that organizations were going to be beating down my door for potential job opportunities. I could not have been any more wrong.

While in NASSAM, I received a few friendly emails from Kai saying that she was hoping that everything in the program was going well and she would like to hear about my experiences when I came back to the U.S. The emails were nonthreatening, and I assumed that I was over the fantasy and that I could actually engage in normal conversations with her. I met her for drinks within the first week of my arrival back home, and the games began all over again. Only this time, engaging in such acts created a hurricane that almost led to my death, pushed me to do things that I never would have imagined doing, and created a lack of job opportunities for me. My biggest fear had been realized—I think I actually made God mad.

Let me begin by telling the first almost-fatal story. As I have previously mentioned, my mental state was completely frazzled. Not in the sense that I was unable to focus and do well in school and at work, but I no longer had a strong sense of right and wrong. I felt that breaking one of the Ten Commandments was the worst possible sin ever, so everything else was trivial in my mind. One evening, while at the boxing gym, a man approached me and asked if I wanted to make a little bit of money on the side. "Absolutely" was my answer. I did not even ask what the job was because I was broke and needed money. He asked me to deliver a package for him, and I agreed. I have no idea what was in the package, but the drop-off location was so close that there was no risk of being stopped by the police because it was within walking distance.

The first delivery was a success. I met this cat after boxing practice for a couple of weeks and delivered small items. It's not like I was moving bricks or anything, so the fear of any major negative consequences to my actions were limited at best. I was boxing, my hand game was nice, and I was not afraid of anybody running up on me with the idea of stealing something from me. I never knew the man's name, and he never knew mine. Sun Tzu said it best when he noted, "Secrecy, misdirection, denial, and deception are keys to the art of war." I was in a war, and I knew it. I just figured that as long as I could stay under the radar, I would be good. That would have been true if I could have stayed under the radar.

One evening about eight blocks away from the boxing gym, I dropped off a package of goods, but the recipient did not want to make payment and began acting reckless. This day and delivery was no different than any other day or delivery, except for the fact that I had a boxing teammate with me. The man refused payment and began to throw punches. I am not sure why he chose to engage in such ignorance, especially considering the fact that he was about 5'7" and about 145 lbs. His actions led to a negative reaction on our part, and let's just say that he did not walk away from the altercation without any bumps and bruises. Kind of like O'Dog and Kain in *Menace II Society,* Speedy and I knew that we were going to have to deal with him in the future, but we just did not know when.

Anyway, that moment came sooner than I anticipated. Well, actually in this case, I was guilty by association. One night while sitting in class, I decided that I was done playing the delivery boy game. I went to the spot where I knew the man would be in order to tell him that I was done. When I arrived, it looked like he had just been ran over by a semi-truck. Both of his eyes were black, his lip was busted and his nose was broken, and he had a gash across the top of his head. Something went wrong that night, and he suffered the consequences. Someone was gunning for him, and my ignorance almost got me killed. While standing there talking, four gunshots rang out. Neither one of us ran because in that area, it was the norm. It did not become real until I realized gunshots five, six, and seven were meant for the guy I was talking to. To hear the sound of a bullet whizzing past someone's head and then hitting something else is inexplicable. I ran in the complete opposite direction of the dude and decided I would pick my car up later. No one knew my name or what I really looked like, so I knew that I was in the clear. Even the guy who had the misfortune of having to deal with two boxers did not really know what I looked like because it was dark outside at the time of the altercation. To be so close and yet so far away from imminent danger is/was a familiar but different experience. It felt exhilarating and scary all at the same time. A few hours later, I walked back to my car and drove home. Charley Escobar had called it quits.

It was very clear to me that trying to make money fast was not the best alternative for me, so I began applying for jobs. If someone would have told me when I first began graduate school that it was going to be hard for me to get a job, I would have told them that they were crazy. In my mind, getting a job was the least of my worries. I was more concerned with the idea of how was I going to decide which job to take. My grades were phenomenal and I had made several contacts through a variety of networking events, so there was nothing inside of me that believed it was going to be a hard process.

I wanted to work at Nike, particularly on the Jordan Brand sports marketing team. A few high-level individuals from Notre Dame opened the door for me to visit the Nike campus and interview for a position on the marketing team. I had ten informational interviews over the course of two days and did extremely well. I was taken by complete surprise on the tenth interview when I realized a black man, in a position of power, was going to stop the whole process. This was my first real situation in which someone who should have been there to help me fly actually cut off my wings. Nine out of the ten interviewers agreed that I was an excellent candidate for employment at Nike and when I was closer to completing my graduate studies, a job would be there for me.

The man who, in my mind sabotaged the process, told me that it was hard to get on any sports marketing team. He questioned why I thought just because I had people from Notre Dame call the bosses that I should be treated any differently. He, in an indirect manner, told me that he was not interested in hiring some kid who happened to know how to interview well. I will paraphrase his words: "You are from the inner city, and you have figured out a way to charm and get every interviewer here on your side, but it will not work on me. I hope you understand that."

Wow. To hear that from someone who should have been cheering me on and encouraging me to do better was surreal. I played his words over 1000 times and could not understand why he would say that. Nine extraordinary interviews and one fantastic interview with a man who had a chip on his shoulder terminated the entire process. He had the most power in the group and ultimately had to sign off on anyone who was hired, so there was really nothing I could do. I just hoped that he would change his mind by the time I graduated and offered me a job within the sports marketing team, but that did not happen. Oh well. I had to move on.

At this point in the story, Kai and I were back on "Fantasy Island" and the frequency of encounters was much higher than in the recent past. I am still not sure how she managed to get away so often and for so long, but she definitely figured out a way. Her husband was probably off doing the same thing she was doing, so he probably was not worried about her whereabouts. Anyway, I digress—back to the story. Kai and I were "playing the game" everywhere: upstairs, downstairs, on the floor, in the shower, at the movie theater. Yes, I said it, at the movie theater, sitting on the back row. *Borat* was a pretty funny movie when I actually watched it later that year.

We had planned a little "getaway" trip for the weekend after the Fourth of July just to add to the adventure and make the story even better. She came over to my house on the Fourth of July night, and that was the last time we made fireworks. Our weekend trip never happened, though, because of my second near-death encounter.

On the morning of 5 July, I had to be at work relatively early to interview a potential intern. I woke up and prepared for my day as usual. Only this time when I went to my car, I noticed one of the tires was severely disproportioned. I took the car into the Honda dealership to get the tire fixed, and as I was driving down the street with my brand new tire, the accident happened. I was driving down the street, and a man who was trying to beat the light and make a left turn T-boned me while driving at a high rate of speed. Luckily, my reaction time was fast and I anticipated the hit, but the impact was still quite damaging. The officer told me that if someone would have been in the passenger seat, the impact would have probably killed that person immediately. He also told me that if I would not have angled the car the way that I did to avoid the collision, I would have been knocked into oncoming traffic and probably seriously injured, if not killed.

God had other plans, though. He was teaching me a lesson, and I knew it. He had given me several warnings, and I did not heed His advice. As a matter of fact, I did the exact opposite. This time though, the message was loud and clear: "Stop, or I will stop you." I was at a crossroads and face-to-face with the enemy known as me. My little cousin wrote a blog called "face-to-face," and it so perfectly describes what I experienced that I will detail it below:

> He's right on my heels and breathing down the back of my neck.
>
> I'm running so fast to the point where I become breathless.
>
> Trying to get to some roots, but too afraid of digging up a painful past so I become restless.
>
> I slow down to get an understanding through communication but I become speechless.
>
> Running from him has caused me to hide from my destiny.
>
> Not only that but I was lacking in integrity.

I found myself straddling over fences of fear and crossing rivers of doubt.

I tried to obtain my purpose to find a way out, but I guess while I was running I dropped it.

I climbed a mountain of false hope only to see that he had already beaten me there.

He looked at me and asked me how do I expect him to breath with no air, but I turned and said I'm the one suffocating, but he said he didn't care.

We were talking from a distance so I couldn't quite see who he was.

He said he knew me better than the hatred that rejected love.

That statement startled me so I took off running again.

He started yelling out my secrets I hadn't even told my closest friend.

He seduced me because of intimidation and raped me with manipulation.

So I'm wondering, who is this man?

I ran down this dark road so he couldn't see me so he started screaming out my name.

I hid behind the shadow of the almighty and there is where the Lord revealed the other person's name.

And to my surprise, BAM!!!!! It was somebody I knew all my life, and all along the person I had been running from was me so I knew it was time to fight.

SCARS, EXILE, AND VINDICATION

Suddenly it was heavy breathing on my face and I wanted to take off running again, but I had been running all my life so I had to stop this race.

Suddenly daylight broke and there we stood, face-to-face. We were as connected as my spirit is to my flesh. It was a point in my life that had to have its resurrection.

Wait... Now what am I going to do?

As I stared into those bold peaceable eyes, I saw smiles but behind it were soft cries.

I saw a brain full of potential and bright future but it was also pumped full of promised lies.

What I saw was a little boy who was trying to get someone to help him catch up to this grown man. On one side there was relief but on the other end was grief.

Not grief that he had lost his mother or never had his father, but the fact that he's a grown man and still doesn't know who he is.

I see a lot of questions that remain unanswered. I sense nourishment but he's also too pressured. He uses his attitude as a weapon and his bitterness as a way of life.

I witnessed death but still he was fighting against the qualities of life.

Beyond the eyes was a person laying hands and they weren't dirty.

But he pulled back and because of hypocrisy not only in himself but others, he felt unworthy.

Judged because his character wasn't fully developed, he knew he was gifted but he fought in a world outside of reality.

So many people said they accepted him into their family, but yet he felt like an orphan. So to him friendlessness was nothing.

Emptiness now has become a self-evaluation, standing on the edge, tempting to jump.

I recognized that he had the understanding that it did not take a slap in the chest or three hours on the floor just to get in God's Presence.

He knows it can be as simple as 10-minute prayer and a life full of benevolence.

I see such confidence but to his knowledge, it is cockiness.

As we look at one another, it's like the deeper I see, the clearer it gets, but at the same time the cloudier it looks.

This was one of the ugliest but purest faces I had ever seen.

Now don't get too spiritual because none of us are all that clean.

The question he struggles with is "why after all of these years Prophet Thomas is just now dealing with Charles Thomas?"

But what he realizes is that a lot of people he's come in contact with haven't dealt with their real self or face-to-face.

So now to this day he still stares me in the face but the solution is this:

I have told all of this, so that no one can expose any of it, but now I have to not only look at it and face it but actually deal with it: Face 2 Face

                Prophet Thomas 2 Charles Thomas.

My relationship with Kai was over, I had dealt with me face-to-face, and now it was time to bounce back.

RESILIENCE: BOUNCE BACK

According to Merriam-Webster, the definition of resilience is, "an ability to recover from or adjust easily to misfortune or change." Simply stated, I define resilience as one's ability to bounce back. Confucius, in one of his many profound statements, commented that, "Our greatest glory is not in never falling, but in rising every time we fall." His words were my source of inspiration on many occasions. I thought that once the Kai saga was over, it was going to be smooth sailing. I was wrong on all accounts. Over the next eight months, I became the king of resiliency—masterful in the art of bouncing back.

After the car accident, I knew it was time to take a look at my life and make a change for the better. I knew that it was not going to be easy, but I had to try. I was not sure how to proceed, but I knew that if I took the first step, God would take care of the rest. School was drawing to a close, and the time had come to begin the job search. My grades were fantastic, I had a laundry list of contacts who vowed to help me if I ever requested their assistance, my résumé was exemplary (or so I thought), and I was a hard worker. In my mind, there was absolutely no reason that I would not be able to secure a high paying job with a top-tiered company. I had experienced one setback with Nike but viewed it as a learning experience and did not allow it to slow me down. Since working at Nike was no longer a viable option, I was able to focus my attentions elsewhere. F. Scott Fitzgerald said, "The test of first-rate intelligence is the ability to hold opposing ideas in mind simultaneously and retain the ability to function. One should be able to recognize that things are seemingly impossible and yet be determined to make them otherwise." That test came and was, for me, a very hard life lesson.

Initially, I wanted to find a job on my own and not call on any of the people who so adamantly stated that they would help me however possible. I put my résumé on careercentral.com, monster.com, and a myriad of other employment websites. I received a host of emails and phone calls from potential employers expressing their interest. However, many of these companies wanted me to do an internship, which I had no interest in doing, or work for a salary that was drastically under market value. I did not want to sell myself short; I did not think I was going to have to do such a thing and considered many of the offers insulting. I made double the salary proposed by some companies before I had a master's degree, so logically, accepting such an offer did not make sense to me. I engaged potential employers on my own for about the first month, but only seemed to get calls from corporations in which I had little to no interest. I was completely confused at how my situation was turning out. I could not understand why none of the big corporations were returning my calls or emails. I had done everything I was supposed to do, and it all seemed to be for naught.

I chose not to let it get to me, though. I knew that I had to remain positive. I learned from Jack Canfield in his book, *The Success Principles*, that our thoughts shape our actions, and event + response = outcome. I knew that I did not have any control over the events that took place, but I did have absolute control over the responses and thus the outcome. I had to be resilient. I did not have a choice. Therefore, instead of getting upset when I received calls from small start-up firms offering me $30K per year, I viewed it as if they knew that I could help their company, but I still respectfully declined the offer and kept moving forward. I was living by the laws of attraction. It became harder and harder to maintain such a positive outlook on life when things were seemingly going so bad for me. I had to put my pride aside and enlist the help of others.

I called basketball coaches, high-level collegiate athletic administrators, CEOs, COOs, lawyers, salespeople, doctors, television producers, director-level friends, friends of friends, etc. I described to them the type of work I was interested in, and they began to make their phone calls. Within two weeks, the phone began ringing off the hook—AT&T, Verizon, Johnson and Johnson, Pfizer, Merck, Gatorade, Adidas, Division I Universities, Goldman Sachs, and Bank of America, to name a few. I was excited, confident, and felt it was finally going to happen. I was going to get a high-paying job in a field of my choice and be able to help the family without any financial strain or complications. The economy was doing well, employers were looking for highly qualified candidates who could make an immediate impact in particular areas of operation, and I felt I was the guy who could do that. *Let the games begin,* I thought.

I had approximately twenty-five phone interviews with top-level organizations and approximately fifty face-to-face interviews over the course of the next six months. Failure is not even an accurate term to describe how I felt. Talk about being able to bounce back and becoming the king of resiliency. I began to feel that the ramifications of being involved in marital infidelity were still looming large. I felt as if God was punishing me. The accident was simply a wake-up call, a warning if you will, for the next storm that I was going to have to endure.

Money was running short, and I had a mortgage to pay. I learned from previous life experiences that involving myself in questionable activities was not a viable alternative and could only lead to more terror and internal destruction. I had to figure out something, and I had to do it fast. I was at a loss; for the first time in my life, I was in panic mode. My thinking was purely survival-oriented. Looking back on the situation, I now understand that my problems seemed so big because at that point in my life, God had become small. Allow me to continue telling you the story.

The streets were calling me to participate in less than legal activities. I knew I could do it and make money, but the danger involved was a major deterrent. In addition, I no longer wanted to compromise my character and/or integrity. So what did I do? I figured out a way to use the educational system for my benefit. I had taken out all of the student loans that I could, and I did not want to get a private loan from the bank. The interest was too high and I would have had to jump through too many unnecessary hoops. I knew I had family members in school so, in an effort to get some sort of financial assistance, I asked my sister if she would apply for the loan for me. Her initial response was yes; I was a fool for believing her. As a matter of fact, I should have never asked her for help because I knew she wasn't going to follow through. But I digress. I filled out all of the paperwork including her school name, major, estimated date of completion and everything else necessary to get the loan. The loan application was tentatively approved, and all I needed was for her to give me a school enrollment verification letter. Three weeks went by, and my funds were getting lower and lower. I asked her about it, and she told me, "Oh yeah, my bad, I will get it for you." I could sense the deception. As I suspected, she was not enrolled.

I was disappointed and hurt by her actions once again. I was not really surprised, though, because she had a history of lying and not following though on her word. I had more of a "Wow, I can't believe I let her do it to me again" feeling. I know she is my sister and all, but at that point I knew that I could no longer trust anything she said to me, and I no longer had a reason to talk to her. I had to rescind the application until further notice. I was not sure if my cousin would let me use his name in an effort to use the educational system to get more money, but I had to try. I called him and his mom and before I could even finish explaining, they had already said yes. I was more than grateful. At least I knew I would have some relief to hold me over for a short time. I was not sure how long, but even a few months was better than nothing. All I had to do was re-apply and hope for the best. I sent in another application; but this time, the educational system was not in such a giving mood. There was a 40 percent reduction from the previous amount. I was not sure why, but I assumed it was because they saw that I never received appropriate documentation for the first loan approval. The amount of money given was not a significant amount, but it was helpful nonetheless.

Once the money was in my account, I was able to breathe easier. I was still swimming against the current, but at least I was not drowning. I paid some bills, sent some money home, and put the rest in the bank to pay more bills. The future was very uncertain at this point, but I refused to let that be a deterrent. *As long as I breathe, there is hope*... that's what I kept telling myself. I began applying for more jobs all across the country. If you recall, I mentioned earlier that I had a surfeit of interviews. My résumé was everywhere, from established Fortune 500 companies to start-ups. I became so adept at the art of interviewing that even some interviewers would compliment me by saying that I was one of the best interviewees they had met in quite some time. I would graciously accept the compliment and then proceed to receive a rejection letter via mail/email within the next couple of weeks. I could not understand where and how I was messing up. My résumé had been professionally written, the interviews were going well, and I seemed to have connected to those in positions of authority. I respectfully declined some job offers because the salary presented was unacceptable, and I simply wanted the interview experience to prepare for higher-level organizations. I was told by some organizations that I was overqualified and by others that they were unable to pay the requested salary amount. All the answers given to me by organizations did not give me any closure, and I felt as if they were all excuses.

I began to doubt myself and wonder if all of the educational training I received was in vain. I then began to contemplate the significance of race and what impact it had on the interview process. Family and friends would say that top-tiered organizations were intimidated when they saw a young black man who was well-educated, well-traveled, eloquent, charming, and articulate; well, I added in the "eloquent, charming, and articulate part," but you understand my point. I listened to their words but took it with a grain of salt; they were supposed to say those things to make me feel better about the situation. I still believed that I was doing something wrong. I have never been one to blame others for my circumstances, and I d*** sure was not going to start now. My thought processes were wrong, my responses to different events in my life were faulty, I was not as adept at the art of answering interview questions as I thought, or maybe the educational background and work experience really did not matter and who I knew was the most important. I did not know what to think. All I knew was that I had to figure it out and figure it out fast.

I began a journey of self-reflection that proved to be extremely difficult, but extraordinarily beneficial. I began to focus on my strengths and asked myself, *When did I excel the most and why? What activities fatigued me? What relationships needed to be priorities in my life?* The last question was the easiest to answer. I had many relationships and tried to make them all top priorities in my life. There were some people that did not have my best interests at heart that I still allowed to influence me. I shouldn't have even been friends with them. I was focusing on every relationship except the one relationship that could have made all the others thrive—my relationship with God. I had not lost my faith, I was not worshipping idol images, and I most certainly had not turned to the dark side. I simply had not put Him first in every decision and allowed His will to take precedent, and He was not at the center of every relationship. I was trying to do things my way and handle problems that I should have passed on to Him. I allowed certain people, also known as "friends," to take advantage of my kindness, and I had lost sight of what was most important in my life—my relationship with God and my family.

When I was feeling somewhat down and out, a friend sent me a message. I am not sure if she wrote it or if someone sent to her. All I know is that it came right on time and helped me keep things in perspective. The message she sent me was this:

> Not everyone is holy enough and healthy enough to have a *front row* seat in your life.
>
> There are some people in your life that need to be loved from a distance. It's amazing what you can accomplish when you let go, or at least minimize your time with draining, negative, incompatible, not going anywhere relationships, friendships, fellowships and family!
>
> Observe the relationships around you: Which ones encourage and which ones discourage?
>
> When you leave certain people, do you feel better or feel worse?
>
> Which ones always have drama or don't really understand, know, and appreciate you and the gift that lies within you?
>
> The more you seek growth, peace of mind, love and truth around you, the easier it will become for you to decide who gets to sit in the *front row* and who should be moved to the balcony of your life.
>
> *You cannot change the people around you ... but you can change the people you are around!*

Ask *God* for wisdom and discernment and choose wisely the people who sit in the *front row* of your life.

Remember that *front row* seats are for special and deserving people and those who sit in the *front row* should be chosen carefully.

Don't let someone become a priority in your life, when you are just an option in theirs. Relationships work best when they are balanced.

I knew I had to change my ways if I wanted to get and stay blessed. It was necessary for me to change acquaintances, associates, and friends.

After reorganizing priorities and focusing on the right relationships, I felt better about my options moving forward. I refused to let a few minor setbacks slow me down. I had endured much worse and had come out victorious, so I knew this was just another character test. I spoke to no less than 100 different people before finally getting a job at a health and fitness center and even that was not easy. I had to go through three different interviews before being offered a full-time, 100 percent commission-based sales job. I could not believe how limited my options were at the time. I could take that job, or continue the internship and earn a salary of approximately $30,000. Neither was a flattering offer, especially considering the fact that my starting salary at the federal government after the completion of my undergraduate degree was higher than that. How could it be that someone who graduated from a nationally ranked and recognized MBA program with a 3.9 GPA had to accept a 100 percent commission-based job selling gym memberships? Was it meant to be a learning experience? Did I miss something in my educational training that would manifest itself as a result of learning to become a better salesman? Was the economy really entering a recession? I had no idea what I was supposed to learn, but I figured I would just roll with it and be the best salesman at the health and fitness center.

It did not take long for me to understand the computer systems as well as all of the services and products that the fitness center had to offer. I quickly excelled and became the top salesman at my location. I was also ranked in the top 5 percent in the state of Texas. That being said, I was still disappointed in myself and knew that I was better than my current situation. My coworkers were cool and it was fun being in a sports-like environment, but I knew that I was not supposed to be there. When customers would ask me if I attended college, I would say no because every time I told someone that I had an MBA, they would look at me like I was crazy and ask why I was selling gym memberships. It became easier not to reveal such information.

I completely committed to the job while simultaneously looking for better employment. I began reading sales books, persuasion books, influence books, management books, and anything else that would allow me to get better at closing deals. "Either be good, get good, or give up" became my philosophy. I figured since I was there, I might as well be the best. I knew that I already had a natural ability to connect to people on a personal level because of my vast array of life experiences, and I also knew the product and service offerings, so speaking confidently and asking for the sale was not a problem. I actually enjoyed watching people do a one-eighty. They would be adamant about not purchasing a membership, and I relished in the challenge of being about to persuade them to do otherwise. My conversion rate hovered the 80 percent mark during my last two months of employment at the fitness center. Nice accomplishment, right? For some people, yes. Me, not even close. Complacency is not it my nature and while I was doing decently well, I knew I had to move on.

HELP FROM ALL THE WRONG, BUT RIGHT, PLACES

As a child, I always assumed that if times turned tough, family and friends would have your back. Unfortunately for me, my family did not have the financial resources to make my transition from graduate school to corporate America easy, so I did not expect much. All I wanted, which I knew they would provide, was love, patience, and support. I did, however, hope that some of the people I considered "friends" would help me along in my journey. Many of my "friends" had high-paying jobs within Fortune 100 companies. A large majority of them even had high-level influence within their respective functional units, and I figured that our relationships were strong enough that helping me out in my time of need would have been a no-brainer. I never directly asked for their assistance, but they knew I was working at a gym and way below my potential. Maybe because I wanted to see all people succeed and enjoyed watching others smile, I was naïve in my friendship characterizations. I will not even mention their names because it is not worth it. I will, however, detail how God sent five angels to help me. Those five angels restored my faith in humanity.

I met Mr. Marpoe in my capstone course while completing my MBA. The capstone course was the final course that I had to take before graduating, and Mr. Marpoe was brought in as a guest speaker. He was a very interesting man. He held high-level titles within top-tiered organizations but grew tired of the rat race and ventured out on his own to become an entrepreneur. He was humorous, intelligent, witty, articulate, focused, determined, driven, and any other adjective that you can think of that might be necessary to become a successful entrepreneur. He spoke to us for about two hours detailing his life experiences, talking about his unwillingness to conform to the rules of corporate giants, and his desire to live at his own pace.

During his presentation, he said, "Many of you are prisoners in your own mind, and only you can stop you from being successful and living the life that you envisioned as a child."

His words struck a chord with me during that presentation and became even more poignant during my inability to secure gainful employment. I had lunch and dinner with Mr. Marpoe on several occasions because I wanted his advice and wanted to learn from someone who was already where I wanted to be. He turned me on to books written by Jack Canfield, Stephen Covey, Malcolm Gladwell, John Maxwell, Donald Clifton, and Marcus Buckingham, etc. He spoke words of encouragement that would prove to be prophetic in my life. God sent Mr. Marpoe to me so that I could see that my circumstances could never define me unless I allowed them to. Mr. Marpoe did not have anything handed to him, either. He fought for it just like I was fighting for it, and his success gave me hope and reason to believe that I could make it as well.

I read every book that he suggested and implanted many of the philosophies and tenets set forth in those books into my life. My period of introspection was enlightening and evolutionary. God sent one man to a class of fifty people to speak to one person. I never gave Mr. Marpoe my résumé, and I never asked him to help me find a job. That was not his purpose. He was not sent to help me find employment. He was sent to help me find me.

His words, willingness to listen, and ability to impart wisdom on someone who was striving for the better things in life afforded me the opportunity to become a better person. I am grateful and thankful to him. Once again, God did not send me someone I wanted and expected. He sent me the person He wanted to send: a middle-aged white man with a desire to teach, motivate, and inspire.

Anna, a beautiful, talented, sweet, and caring former NFL cheerleader went above and beyond the call of duty to help me find a job. I met Anna through a mutual friend who told me to call her when some friends and I were going to Miami for vacation. The very first time I called her, we had an immediate connection and talked for over an hour. When I finally met her in person, it was as if we had been friends forever. The conversation was easy, and laughter was not forced. We hung out quite a bit during my vacation and while there was potential to start a relationship other than a friendship, the long distance made it difficult, if not impossible. Either way, she was another godsend.

Unbeknownst to me, Anna was well-connected in many circles—from media and entertainment agencies to law firms and corporate giants. She knew an assortment of people and was willing to introduce me to all of them. She called many of her contacts, sent emails, texted them, and did whatever else she could think of to contact them. She did not have to and, quite frankly, I do not know why she did. She was sent to be a blessing to me. God bestowed His grace, His unmerited favor, upon me through her. Anna sent my résumé to more people and firms than I can count. Although I did not get a job through her contacts, her efforts were well-received, and I am more than appreciative of her. She is a wonderful person to do what she did and I want her to know, from the bottom of my heart, I am thankful. Anna also gave me reason to believe that I was bigger than my circumstances. Because of her efforts, I knew that through sheer determination and an unwillingness to back down, I would be all right.

Once again, I flooded the Internet with my résumé. I sent it to pharmaceutical companies, sports companies, medical device sales organizations, casinos, hospitals, and the list goes on. However, my résumé was a little more focused and streamlined this time. It was shorter, the objective was clearer, the wording was more powerful, and the ordering made more sense. I was confident that this résumé would elicit more responses and hopefully a plethora of interviews with reputable organizations. I prayed for the best.

Sure enough, my prayers were answered. My cell phone was inundated with calls from hiring managers of top-tiered organizations. The only problem, which was a good problem, was figuring out how to schedule the interviews without rocking the boat at my current place of employment. Amazingly, God knows what He is doing way before we even know what could potentially happen. It just so happened that my work schedule did not begin until 11:00 a.m. or noon, and I had Wednesdays off. My only early start was Saturday, and that did not matter because I knew that I would not have any interviews on Saturday anyway. I figured I would be able to fly out on a Tuesday night after work, interview all day Wednesday, fly out Wednesday night, and be back at home to start my 11:00 a.m. or noon shift on Thursday. It worked out perfectly.

While reading an entrepreneur magazine at Barnes and Nobles one evening, I started a conversation with a gentleman who was reading a tattoo magazine. I am a fan of human artwork and figured he might know of some upcoming tattoo conventions. While we were talking, he began to randomly ask me about my career goals and aspirations. I was moderately thrown off by his line of inquiry, particularly since I asked him about tattoos and nothing even remotely career-oriented. During the conversation, he asked me if I was interested in sales, specifically pharmaceutical sales. I told him that I was interested in sales and that my résumé was probably with every pharmaceutical sales company in North America. He laughed, told me that he was a district manager, and advised that I send him my résumé. As requested, I sent Mr. Scott my résumé that very same night. I thought he was going to be like everyone else and just talk the talk without walking the walk. I was pleasantly surprised when I heard from one of his hiring managers within a week. They were extremely impressed with my résumé, and I was also advised that I made a very good impression on Mr. Scott—good thing he liked tattoos. The hiring manager told me that I was a top candidate for a field rep position and was to be interviewed ASAP. The following week, I flew to Atlanta on a Tuesday night and prepared to interview all day Wednesday.

The first interview was a panel of seven employees who all asked different behavioral-type questions to better understand my line of thinking and ability to answer questions succinctly while still being specific. I had studied the company and knew a variety of products and how they could positively and/or negatively impact the customer. I was very prepared and even had questions for them. The panel interview was actually quite fun. I looked it at it as being more of a performance. I considered them to be the judges whom I had to woo and get on my team. An hour later, the panel interview was over, and it was time for the real tests; I had five more one-on-one interviews. I knew the interviews would be much more focused, and I had to be on my A-game. "Let's play ball" was my reaction. I will not bore with the details of each individual interview, but I did well and I knew it. I answered questions appropriately and knew when to interject in order to ask questions. Five hours later the game was over, and I had a triple-double. There was no doubt in my mind that I would be offered the job. They had three more candidates to interview, but I was not worried. I did my best, so all I could do was wait.

As I was walking back into the hotel after an exhaustive day of interviews, a man in front of me dropped a stack of papers, and one of the papers I handed him was a business card. The card indicated that he was a medical devices salesman—angel number four—Mr. Jacobson. I told him how interested I was in such a field but had no contacts to guide me through the process. We sat down and had dinner that night, and he requested a résumé. Since I had extras from my earlier interviews, I gave him one on the spot. People always say be careful what you wish for because it just might come true. I asked to be bombarded with calls and interviews. I wanted to go on a surplus of interviews because I wanted to have options. I felt that my academic and professional work record spoke for itself so I should have had options to choose from and not have to take a job out of desperation.

Mr. Jacobson was true to his word; and the next day while I was working, I received a call from a human resources representative. I informed the HR rep of my work situation and advised that the soonest I could be in Michigan was the following Wednesday. She was agreeable, and the following Tuesday night, I was in Michigan preparing for my Wednesday interviews. The hiring manager advised me that the interviews would be behavioral in nature as well as company-focused, so it was important to have concrete examples of past professional and academic successes as well as know fundamental foundational information in regards to the company. These interviews were similar to the interviews that took place in Atlanta, except the ordering was reversed, there were more one-on-one interviews, and the panel consisted of nine individuals.

In my opinion, the first interview did not go so well. I have no excuses, but I did not sleep well the night before and, as a general rule, I am not mentally focused to do anything at 7:30 a.m., particularly answer interview questions. I am not sure if the interviewer was tired as well, but his body language and line of questioning did not seem to change when I fumbled through a couple of the company-related questions. Maybe I dodged a bullet and, by 8:15 a.m., I was ready to rock and roll. The next seven interviews were all approximately forty-five minutes in length, and I hit home runs in every one. At the end of each interview, I would ask the interviewer if he/she thought there was any reason that I would not be offered a position within the company. Each person responded that they felt as if I were a perfect fit for the company and as long as I did well in the nine-person panel interview, I would more than likely be offered the position. At approximately 4:00 p.m., it was once again time to perform, and perform I did. It was as if we were salsa dancing together. I was in lockstep with the interviewers. For every question they asked, I had an even better answer. It was like poetry in motion. Again, after one hour, the game was over. My team won, and I had a "double nickel"—a fifty-five point night, as Michael Jordan so eloquently coined it. I got on the plane back to San Antonio, and it was time to play the waiting game. The pharmaceutical company and the medical device company both told me that they would get back to me within a couple of weeks if not sooner, so now I had to be patient.

A few days later, while working out, angel number five called. Mr. Vez was my graduate school counselor and had been an advocate for me since the day I met him. He was always very upbeat and positive when discussing potential job offerings with me, but this day there was more excitement in his voice. He told me to leave the gym, put on a suit, and take my résumé to a career fair. I did not understand why he was so excited about this particular fair because they had all been a complete waste of time for me. He explained that the representatives from an extremely reputable and well-known hotel in Las Vegas were doing on-the-spot interviews for qualified candidates. I was not all that interested in the gaming industry, but since Mr. Vez recommended the company, I decided to check it out.

As I anticipated, the career fair was less than stellar, and the particular hotel he mentioned was not doing on-the-spot interviews. The representatives that I spoke to advised that they were accepting résumés but not doing live, on-the-spot interviews. They told me to find jobs that interested me on their website and post my résumé there as well. I went to the website, but the only available positions were call center, housekeeping, and food and beverage positions. I wanted another job and Vegas seemed like a fun place to live, but I was not even distantly interested in any of the posted positions. I simply posted my résumé in the general section and prayed for the best. I figured if they were interested, someone would contact me. I spoke to Mr. Vez and informed him of the situation. As usual, he was more than optimistic and had more confidence in me that I even had in myself at that point. He told me not to worry, and he was sure something good would happen soon. I was hopeful that he was correct because I needed and wanted a job paying a good salary ASAP.

Two weeks went by and I had not received a phone call or email from anyone about any potential job offerings. I was upset at myself because I could not figure out what I was doing wrong. I, according to the interviewers, had done a phenomenal job at answering and asking questions, so I was confused as to why I had not heard back from anyone. I have learned to take full responsibility and accountability for everything that happens in my life, and I do not give excuses as to why something did not work out in my favor, but I was still in a state of amazement that no one had reached out to me. I remained hopeful and kept telling myself that no news was good news.

You know the saying, "When it rains, it pours"? Well, over the course of the next two weeks, that statement would prove itself to be true. As I was leaving work one night, I received an email saying that a recruiter from a Las Vegas hotel was going to be at school interviewing candidates for executive management training programs, and I had been chosen to participate in the interviews. *About d*** time,* I thought to myself. I knew that I had to prepare myself for the interviews because they were scheduled for two days from the day I received the email. I called the recruiter the next morning and requested an early morning interview so that I could go to work at my normal time and not have to answer any questions in regards to my whereabouts. The interview was scheduled for the following morning at 9:00 a.m., and I began to prepare myself for another behavioral interview, also known as "tell me about a time when" style interview.

The interview went well, and the recruiter called her immediate boss who happened to be the senior vice president of human resources and advised him that she felt that I was the candidate for the job. I was very excited. I was going to finally get a high-paying and fun job, or so I thought. As I was driving to work, the senior vice president called me and said that I must have really impressed the recruiter because she was adamant that he call me and proceed with more follow-up interviews. We set up another round of interviews, but this time they would be in Las Vegas—Sin City. I was ecstatic. Las Vegas. I had not been to Las Vegas since Lana and I went for a short vacation in 2005.

I arrived in Vegas a few days later and as soon as I got off the plane, I felt like I was home. The same "this is where I need to be" feeling that I had on my first visit to San Antonio was there again. I was not sure what to expect, but I was prepared for any and everything. I had studied and learned quite a bit of background information on the organization, and I also knew biographical data on all of the top-level executives. When I picked up my bag, I was greeted by a driver. I knew from conversations with the recruiter that a "car" was going to pick me up, but I was only expecting a regular car—maybe a Mercedes or BMW. Just kidding. By regular car, I mean a taxi. I walked right past the Rolls-Royce, and the driver just began to laugh. Clearly, I did not think that the Rolls was for me.

He said, "Mr. Thomas, where are you going?"

I innocently replied, "I have no idea." When I realized that I was going to be in the Rolls-Royce, I just smiled and thought, *This is what the good life must be like,* and off we went to the resort. I knew that I was there to interview for an executive management/leadership training program, but I was unaware that I was really going to be interviewed by top-level executives within the company. Upon check-in, I received my room assignment, was told that all food and beverage was going to be taken care of for my two-night stay, and was given my itinerary. I was in for an intense two days of interviews. All interviews were slated for one hour. I was to have six interviews on day one with individuals at the director and vice president levels, and five interviews on day two with individuals at the senior vice president and C-suite level. No problem. At this point, I was so well-versed in the art of interviewing that I was actually looking forward to it. Just like back in my sports playing days and in Atlanta for the other interviews, when the lights are on, it is time to perform.

Day one went very well. I was completely impressed by the staff and their professional demeanor and from what I was told, they were impressed with my background, interviewing skills, and desire to succeed in such a competitive market. Although I did well, it was an exhausting day. The interview questions were very specific, and the interviewers wanted specific and detailed answers that signified teamwork and my willingness and ability to lead. I did well, though, and knew that my preparation had served me well.

I was introduced to the Vegas life very quickly. After finishing my last interview, I was walking through the hotel in an attempt to go back to my room when a young woman stopped me. We exchanged pleasantries as well as phone numbers. A few hours later, we had a few drinks; she went back to my room and...use your imagination to tell yourself the rest of the story. Let me just say this, she had a tattoo on the inside of her thigh that was very well done.

Day two interviews went just as well. I met with the chief financial officer, the chief operations officer, and three other senior vice presidents. Again, they were all very welcoming and easy to talk to. The questions were hard, but I think I did a more than sufficient job at appropriately answering those questions. I was somewhat interrupted during the last interview because my phone kept vibrating. It was low enough though that I do not think the interviewer heard it. I was not sure if something had gone wrong at home or what, but it vibrated three consecutive times.

After the interview was over and I was a safe distance away, I checked my phone to see who was calling me and why. I had three missed calls and three email messages. The messages all said the same thing: "We are interested in more interviews and would like you here within a week." I did not know how I was going to make this happen, but I did know I would not be able to come up with an excuse good enough to leave work for five extra days if I went back, so I didn't. I called the job, told them I had family issues to handle, and set up three different interviews in three different states on three different days. I know… crazy, right? I felt like I was living on planes and in airports instead of my house. I just kept telling myself that everything was going to work out fine, and the interviews and exhaustion were only temporary. I was not lucky enough to meet another random Vegas chick on night number two, but it was all good because I was mad tired anyway. The next morning, I flew back to San Antonio in order to wash clothes and prepare for a mid-evening flight.

Over the course of the next five days, I went from the airplane to the hotel to the interview location to the interview room, back to the hotel, and back to the airport for my next flight.. I felt like I was running from the law or in a movie. It was fun and exciting, but also very tiring and mentally draining. Two days after returning to normal life in San Antonio, I was summoned to Vegas once again to interview with one more person. I agreed because

I was more than interested in living and working in Las Vegas at this point. I flew out the next night, interviewed the following day, and was back in San Antonio that same night so I could prepare for work the next day.

As I was preparing for work the next morning, I received three emails from the companies that I previously interviewed with. As I had anticipated and hoped for, all three emails said roughly the same thing: "Mr. Thomas, we sincerely appreciate your interest in our organization and based on our conversations, initiating a working relationship seems to be the logical choice. Please indulge us by accepting an offer of employment with a remuneration package of [dollar amount]." At this point, I was in the driver's seat, and I knew it. I had three job offers from sales- and marketing-related companies and two offers for positions within the office of athletics at two Division 1 universities. I was interested in all five positions, but the idea of living and working in Las Vegas was the most enticing.

I immediately called the recruiter in Las Vegas and apprised her of the situation. I advised her that I was most interested in working for a world-class resort, but I was going to need a decision from the "powers that be" sooner than later. I was intrigued by the notion of being part of an executive-level training program at a world-class hotel/casino in Las Vegas, and the opportunities seemed to be limitless. All of the executives were professional in their dealings with me, they seemed to be knowledgeable, and I had a good feeling that they wanted me to be a part of the team. I was not forceful in my request for a quicker than normal decision, but I was clear in the fact that I had several alternatives to consider. I knew that I only had two weeks to inform the other organizations of my decision to either accept or decline the offer. That being said, I knew that I had to press the issue in a respectful way. I told her that Vegas was my number-one choice, and if she could talk on my behalf, I would be grateful. She advised that she would do her best to expedite the decision-making process and inform the authorities that I was under time constraints and needed a decision within a week.

In an attempt to leave no stone unturned, I called all five alternatives and negotiated salary, vacation days, sick days, outside consulting opportunities, flex time, company stock, 401K options, etc. When it was all said and done, I was secure in the fact that all offers were competitive and I would be in a position to succeed in the future. With one week remaining until I had to make a decision, I received a job offer and an opportunity to live and work in Vegas. To say that I was disappointed in the salary would be an understatement. It was almost an insult. The initial salary conversation went something like this: "Hey Charles. We are very excited to have you join our family. Your skill set, practical work experience, and educational background have placed you in a position to succeed, and we would like to be a part of that success. We would like for you to start in March, and your salary will be $40K." *Are you nuts?* was what I thought in my head, but I maintained my composure.

I asked the HR rep to go back to the VP and advise him that I had requested a much higher salary—$75K—at least something comparable to the other offers. I told them that with my educational background, previous work experience, and potential to do well, $40K was not an acceptable offer to me. When I look back it at now, I do not think I was off base in my assessment of the situation. Within an hour, I was on the phone with the senior vice president of human resources. I thought I was a pretty good salesman but, d***, he was much better and clearly much more experienced. We spoke for about thirty minutes, and he explained to me how he understood that I had several job offers, but he felt that being in an executive management-training program would prove to be extremely beneficial for me in the future. I was advised that the networking opportunities and the potential to become extremely successful as a result of working at a world-class, five-star resort were endless. I was sold on the idea that within six to eight months, I would be promoted to a director-level position and receive a significant salary increase. The SVP told me that since I was so inexperienced in the gaming industry, he would not be able to justify a salary of $75K-$80K. He told me that he could offer me a starting salary of $55K, with much more to come in the very near future. I will not say that I was naïve to executive speak and the business world, but who was I to call him a liar? He seemed to be a pretty honest individual during the interview process, and I thought his word would be his bond.

I was very unimpressed with the salary offer because I made much more than that before earning my MBA. I assumed that being part of such an elite program would prove to be advantageous in the future, and the idea of living in Las Vegas was alluring. However, three of the five job offers were $80K, and the other two salary offers were $60K and $65K. The downside of accepting any of the $80K offers was that promotions were hard to come by; and based on conversations with people doing the job that I was going to be doing, it could take upward of two years before receiving a salary increase other than the customary cost of living increase at the end of the year. I also would not have the opportunity to manage people or projects for at least two years. I was somewhat skeptical of the other two job offers because I was not fully convinced of the economic stability and/or future progress of the companies. I wanted to make money, but I did not want to sacrifice my happiness to do it. I wanted to go to a place where there were significant chances for rapid upward mobility, and I also wanted to be in a place where I could have fun. I knew that living off $55K was going to be tough, but I figured I would only have to endure such hardships for six to eight months—ten maximum—and I would receive a significant salary increase that would make my life much easier.

I was not sure which decision to make, but I knew I had to make a decision. Consequently, I called the other five organizations and respectfully declined their offers. After each phone call,

I felt a bit of anxiety and uncertainty in not knowing if I made the right choice. I could only tell myself that God was on my side, I was making the right choice, and time would make things all right. I advised the SVP of my decision; he congratulated me and welcomed me to the family. Was I ready? Only time would tell. I had five unsuspecting angels give me words of wisdom, guidance, assistance, and encouragement. They believed in me for no real reason, so I had to believe in myself. I made the choice of working for a top-level resort, and I had to be positive. I was off to Las Vegas...

FAITH, DESIRE, PATIENCE

So here I was in Vegas—Sin City. I had to get away from Texas. A brand-new start was necessary. An affair, a probably not-so-legal moneymaking scheme, a host of late night female interactions, and a graduate degree encompassed my time in San Antonio. I probably should have moved to Idaho or Wyoming so that the wild life would not have been such a major temptation, but resisting the temptation was starting to become more fun than actually following though with my worldly desires.

It was in Las Vegas, Nevada, that I began a journey of self-discovery and spiritual enlightenment that transformed the way I viewed myself, others, and everything around me. As Dr. Wayne Dyer so eloquently stated,–"When you change the way you look at things, the things you look at change." My time in San Antonio was rough because God was not first and foremost in my life. I dealt with God as if it was a democracy. He would tell me to do something, but instead of absolute obedience, I would vote and choose to opt out of the plan if it was not in congruence with what I wanted. That was completely wrong. I failed to realize that in a kingdom, there is only one King who reigns supreme. I was going to church every Sunday, but I was not tithing and I was not in tune with my spiritual self. I was merely existing. I wanted echoes and not answers. I was not truly living. I knew that if I did not relinquish my crown and let God lead, Las Vegas was going to be even crazier than San Antonio. I knew that it was not going to be easy, but I knew I had to try. My star player was back in the game, and I knew that He was not going to let me down.

The first few months in Las Vegas were nothing but fun. I knew that I should have been working to do a better job of changing my ways, but it was much more difficult than I initially anticipated. Talking to girls was like adding two plus two over and over again—mind-numbingly easy. There was no skill or gamesmanship involved, and oftentimes the girls approached me. Turning down a well-cooked steak that is handed to you on a platter with apple pie on the side is not as easy as you may think. I am by no means immune from the temptations of life; and for the first few months, I failed repeatedly.

The games actually began at my place of employment. On my second day of work, I met a girl at a casino event. We exchanged pleasantries as well as phone numbers and set up a time to go on a social outing. Two days later, she was at my house, we had a few drinks and...you tell yourself the rest of the story. Anyway, we had exorbitant amounts of fun. We drank, we laughed, we played. We drank, we laughed, we played...you get the picture.

Life was good. I was having fun at work, I was meeting new people on an almost daily basis, and I was engaged in a no-strings-attached, purely physical relationship. I had the freedom to hang out with other girls, do what I wanted to do, and there was nothing that anyone could say about anything because I was not committed to anyone in particular. The highlight of the no-strings-attached relationships occurred on Cinco de Mayo. After about five margaritas, a stint in the hot tub, a couple more margaritas, and a game of strip Go Fish with her and one of her female friends, I had one of the wildest nights of my life. It was not an isolated incident during my first few months in Sin City.

On any given night, it was uncertain as to how the night would end. When in Vegas, do as the people in Vegas do. I lived that life, but quickly tired of it when I felt myself going down the same San Antonio road. I learned from my previous mistakes and refused to relive the same hardships, especially because I did not have to. I knew better. I knew that I knew better so it would have been juvenile of me to continue engaging in acts that were slowly but surely attacking my character and integrity. I was in complete control of my actions, so I stopped. I believe the only way to reasonably predict the future is to invent it. I found a church home, began tithing again, refocused my attentions and prayers to God, stopped messing with all of the girls and, just like that, life got harder. My professional life turned into a complete fiasco. I have faced and overcome many adversities in my life, but to say that all of the odds were stacked against me would be an understatement. Somebody, and I can honestly say that I have no idea who, but somebody began watching my every move.

The first "Are you kidding me?" moment happened on a Saturday afternoon. I came into work on my day off in an effort to show some initiative and get some things done. I walked past the VP of the department's office, and he asked me to come into his office. Cool. No big deal, I wasn't trippin'. He proceeded to tell me that someone told him that I was wearing my earrings on the property. Working in a high-class hotel/resort, I already knew how image conscience people were, so I made a decision not to wear my earrings to work. I questioned the veracity of the statement and reminded him that I never wear my earrings to work. I told him that I went to the nightclub on the property the night before at about 1:00 a.m., and at that point I did choose to wear the earrings that I bought with my money. He told me that I could not wear my earrings at any time while I was on the property. I immediately cut the conversation short and respectfully advised him that I could wear whatever I wanted to wear, however I wanted to wear it, when I was not on the clock. I also told him that with the bull**** salary I was getting paid, no one had the right to microscope my wardrobe unless they had intentions of giving me more money to upgrade. He laughed it off, but I was as serious as a heart attack. Even though it was not a major issue, I could not believe that he would even mention something like that to me. The second "Are you kidding me?" moment occurred on another Saturday afternoon. At this point, I should have known to not go to work on Saturdays because apparently Saturdays were "let's f*** with CT day." I worked for about five hours, and as I was preparing to walk downstairs to get some information to help me complete the task that I was doing, the boss called me into his office. Again, no big deal, until he began talking. His voice was somber this time, and I knew something was wrong. He told me that a coworker had filed sexual harassment against me. I could not believe it because I had not done anything wrong. I asked him to give me details pertaining to the allegation such as who filed the claim, why, about what, etc. He explained to me that someone who I actually considered to be a friend told her boss that I sexually harassed her.

"Nala," I said. How could this be? I was not even mad about the situation; I was more shocked than anything. These allegations came from a girl who I had already been out with in a group setting on several occasions and a few times in a one-on-one setting. We had been to the nightclub together, to a baseball game, to work functions, and to watch NBA play-off games. So I was mystified to hear that she had filed sexual harassment against me. The VP then went on to tell me that she saved an email I wrote her asking her out on a date. I remembered the email, but the email was not dishonorable in any way. To be honest, I was just joking with her and did not think anything of it because we always joked around like that. She would say things to me like, "Hurry up and make some money so you can take care of me," or "If you are lucky, maybe I will watch the game with you tonight." I knew it was all in good fun, so why should I have been offended by such remarks? So to hear that she took something I wrote in an email to her boss was crazy. I really did not even know how to respond. I learned at that moment that it is okay for people to say what they want to say to another person as long as it is not in the form of written communication.

The VP proceeded to tell me that the matter had been escalated to HR and that I was going to have to talk to some people in employee relations. Cool, no problem. I was not the least bit concerned about any potential consequences. I had emails in which she invited me out to functions, pictures that we had taken together, and text messages we sent back and forth to each other. I was still was confused, though. She and I had discussed work-related issues in the past, and I did not take her for the envious type; but the more I thought of it, the more I began to believe that jealousy had taken over. She did not like the fact that I came into the company at a manager-level position and she was working as a performance analyst. I also felt that her racist roommate/coworker had convinced her to participate in such an indiscretion. Her jealousy and discontent with racial equality were blatantly obvious. But I digress. Nala saw an opportunity to take advantage of a situation which she thought would cause me to get into some sort of trouble, and acted illogically. The VP also validated my thought processes when he told me that he knew they were hostile toward me because of my background and prior work experiences, none of which I ever talked to either of them about. It was not my fault that they chose to remain in their current positions. If they felt and/or knew better options were available, they should have pursed those options. I did not, however, feel it necessary nor acceptable to lower my standards of excellence and confess to something I didn't do simply because a few people felt insecure around me. I could not wait to meet with the people in HR and have the opportunity to speak to Nala in person. It was my objective to make her look and feel like a complete idiot. I planned to dominate the conversation and prove to whomever was in the room that her accusations were false and without merit. I had all of the necessary documentation and was ready to proceed. The employee relations counselors who were familiar with the details of my case acted like this situation was above their levels of expertise. Their lines of questioning and elicitation techniques were infantile at best. Not only did I effectively handle and answer their questions in specific detail, but I also questioned them on the basis of their line of inquiry and demanded justifications as to the real reasons such allegations were brought against me. I figured that if they were not willing to answer questions, then they should not ask questions.

As I provided documentation and discussed in detail the level of our "friendship," they seemed to be shocked that she would file such a grievance. At one point, the employee relations manager said to me that it was not actually a sexual harassment case. When I requested that she tell me what type of case it was, she was unable to do so. Again, her inability to follow through with any rational line of logical inquiry proved to be detrimental to her case. Even if she would have taken Nala's side, her ineptitude would not have allowed her to proceed any further than the initial investigation and interview. About one-and-a-half hours later, the "interview" was over. I had presented my case. Unbeknownst to me others had already vouched for my character and integrity. The case was closed and no disciplinary actions were given, and I was advised that I would not be contacted in regards to the case moving forward. God had once again given me the ability to articulate my interests and clear my name of any and all false misrepresentations.

As I look back on it now and engage in self-reflection, I understand that it was probably the right choice to not have us in the same room with each other. Coming from their point of view, the situation could have turned into an argument, and questions could not have been asked or answered objectively. I wanted answers, but was unable to get them from the source, and that was a major reason for my anger. I knew, from the very beginning, that there was much more to the situation than what I was being told, and it was just frustrating to never know the real reasons behind the accusations. It's okay, though. You live and you learn, right?

The above situation may not seem like a big deal in the grand scheme of things and, in actuality, it probably is not. However, in my world, it was not something I was willing to have in my professional file, and I did my best to make sure that did not happen. Other than detailing my version of our "friendship" in a written format, nothing was placed in my file. After the incident was over, my emotions went from surprise and dismay to furious. Not only was I appalled at the fact that she tried to set me up for failure, but now I really believed that her intentions were completely malicious. It was also frustrating to know that management would actually allow such lies to be heard, but I guess they were just doing their jobs and trying to avoid any potential legalities. Oh well. *Control what you can and try not to worry about anything else* was what I kept telling myself. Unfortunately for me, I had been learning things the hard way. They say experience is the best teacher, but it is often times very difficult to understand what lesson is being taught when you are in the middle of the situation.

I was unable to sleep for about one month after the incident occurred. I would go to bed mad every night and would hope that I would see Nala the next day so that I could curse her out one-on-one and really give her something to complain about. I never had the opportunity to do so because I would only see her in professional meetings. My demeanor toward her, however, was no longer cordial. If looks could kill she would have no longer been in existence on several occasions. It still boggled my mind that she would do such a thing. I prayed about it repeatedly but was still unable to sleep. I asked God to forgive me for any perceived indiscretions and bad thoughts against her, and I prayed that God would allow her to forgive me.

It still was not enough, and I could not figure out why. I had sequentially went through phases of emotions—from shock to anger to disbelief to not caring, back to anger to acceptance. It was not until a church service about forgiveness that I realized what I was doing wrong. God spoke to me as clearly as He ever had and told me to forgive her. I had already done everything but that. At that moment I said, "Nala, I forgive you," and suddenly it seemed as if my shoulder blades had just shifted; it was like the greatest gift I could get... the weight had been lifted. In one moment, I wholeheartedly understood that forgiveness was for me and not the other person. By harboring feelings of ill will and resentment toward another, they actually have control over your life. My inability to sleep at night was a direct result of my focus being on an earthly being and not my heavenly Father. When I re-shifted my focus and forgave her, I slept like a baby, and an apology from her was no longer necessary.

In an effort to bury the hatchet, I sent her the following message:

> I really don't know what to say or why I am even giving this to you, but I am sure it will help me sleep better at night because for the last month or so, I haven't been able to do so. Maybe tragedy changes a person's perspective, or maybe it's wisdom. Anyway, I have never been able to stay mad at people for long or hold grudges. Maybe it's not in my nature, or maybe I just don't care that much about certain things that I allow myself to stay angry or upset for prolonged periods of time. Who knows. Although I will probably never understand why it happened, I just wanted to ask you to forgive me for any perceived wrongdoings against you as I have already forgiven you. Life is too short for nonsense and I try to stay as far away from negativity as possible. I learned a long time ago that if I change the way I look at things, the things I look at change. I don't know how you feel about the situation that occurred, or what you think when we cross paths, but I want you to know that I am not mad. It is true that everything happens for a reason, so we just all have to do our best to live freely and learn from it all. I don't usually promise things, but I can promise you this—there are no hard feelings. Hatchet buried.

With that, it was done, and I moved forward.

THE BETRAYAL: ORGANIZATIONAL LOYALTY IS AN OXYMORON

Prior to joining the organization, I was told that I would receive a promotion in six months. I was advised that based on my learning potential and ability to "hit the ground running," a merit- and performance-based promotion seemed reasonable. I came in with a very strong work ethic and a positive outlook. For eight months, I worked six days per week and a minimum ten hours per day. On special event weekends, I would often work twelve-plus hour days. I tried to be a sponge. I asked questions, I made suggestions when necessary, and I did my best to help coworkers. There was nothing in me that said I would not get a promotion if I asked for one, particularly considering the fact that I waited two additional months to even approach the promotion subject. Consequently, I prepared to negotiate. I formulated a list of questions, detailed my list of accomplishments to date, and outlined a list of projects that would enhance revenue as well as departmental morale. I anticipated their responses and had logical rebuttals to those arguments. I negotiated from my perspective as well as the company perspective before setting up the meeting.

I walked into the meeting very well prepared. The VP read my proposal and without an inkling of emotion or concern said, "We can't do it because of economic conditions." I revisited his words and advised him that he told me that I would be eligible for a salary increase and potential title change in six months. I spoke to him about my list of accomplishments and potential to do even more with the proper guidance and interdepartmental support. He could not come up with a valid excuse other than economic conditions would not allow him to grant my request. Mind you, four executive-level casino hosts with high salaries in my department had been fired, and no one was replaced. I was not asking for $100K, I just felt as if $55K was unacceptable. Even with a $20K increase, I would have still been below the salaries of the individuals whom were recruited under similar conditions as myself. I could not believe that he used the economy as a crutch. I was disappointed, but I showed no emotions or signs of weakness. I just knew that I would no longer put in that type of effort if being rewarded was not even an option. I walked out of his office and knew that the VP did not care about my personal or professional growth.

If you can recall, I told you the story earlier in this chapter about someone telling the VP that I wore my earrings to the nightclub on the property. If you think that was crazy, keep reading. Apparently, I did the wrong thing in trying to validate my value and potential within the company because, for whatever reason, someone began watching me like a hawk. My every move was scrutinized. In management classes, professors teach a theory called the "halo effect." In essence, the "halo effect" occurs when a person is viewed as being able to do no wrong. If you walk by and they are not at their desk, you assume they are in a meeting or in a training session. Well I was the opposite, apparently. Someone was out to get me, and it became his or her sole objective to do so. I was never approached directly by anyone; I would just hear things through the grapevine. I would be on my phone talking to a customer while walking to the bathroom, and someone would tell the director of my department that they saw me talking on the phone in the hallway. I was advised one time that someone saw me sending a text message and smiling at the same time, so I could not have possibly been talking to a customer about hotel accommodations. The best one was when I was told that someone saw me standing up at my desk and laughing while talking on my work phone, so they were sure I was on a personal call. I did not event get mad; I simply told the director to tell whomever they had watching me to talk to me in person if they had a problem. She became defensive and gave me the "don't kill the messenger" speech. There was no way that I was going to let people who were hiding in the shadows steal my joy. The fact that I laughed when she told me such nonsense made the situation worse, I think. Either way, I knew that I was doing a good enough job to not be harassed on a daily basis, and there was nothing anyone could say to deny it. I even went as far as telling the VP that if I ever found out who the confidential informant was, we were going to have a public display of misunderstanding. I did not hear about another complaint.

A couple of weeks went by with nothing new happening. No one was hawking me, I had not had to go to HR for anything, and our department was doing well. I know, right...a miracle. There must have been some kind of machine that read my thoughts and relayed that information to the "powers that be" within the organization, because as soon as I thought that, two more curve balls were thrown at me. Good thing I have phenomenal hand-eye coordination and was able to smack both balls out of the park.

The first curve ball caught me completely off guard. I was told by a third party, yet again, that the same senior vice president who told me that he was extremely impressed with my work, work ethic, and ability to catch on did not like the fact that I was in another graduate school program. He told the director, who told me, "Why does he want to be so educated?" Wow. Maybe so I would not say ignorant things like that. He was one of those guys who started at the bottom, met the right people with money, and slowly but surely was given a senior vice president position even though he should not have been afforded such opportunities.

The second curve ball came during the Christmas holiday season. We had a meeting on Dec 24th, and no one explicitly advised me that it was necessary for me to come in on Christmas Day. Considering it was a very slow time period, I figured that I did not have to work. On December 26th, I walked into a firestorm. The director asked me to come into her office and then began telling me how I was supposed to be at work on Christmas Day. She told me that the VP advised her that a "no call, no show" was grounds for termination. I calmly told her that no one advised me that I needed to be at work on Jesus' birthday and reminded her that neither she, nor the VP worked that day either, so why should I have had to come. I told her if she felt that she could terminate me for that, by all means, be my guest. I also told the VP that if he wanted me to work on the 25th, he should have told me instead of saying see you on the 26th. It was just a miscommunication, but you would have thought that I tried to rob the place and everybody in it. Oh well, as usual, problem solved.

The dust settled, and the sun continued to rise and shine on its own. I was doing my job, but still thinking of ways to get out. I felt as if I was being targeted for no apparent reason. I did not feel as if I was a part of the team and, most importantly, I felt like I was losing brain power as the days progressed. I had to hold off, though. The economy was bad, most organizations were in panic mode, and new career opportunities were scarce. While the world was in a violent storm, I was at peace. God had me where He wanted me. The reasons were not clear to me, but I learned at an early age to view everything as a learning experience. Church and my interactions with people in the church were keeping me grounded. During my journey of spiritual enlightenment and personal growth, I decided it was important to invite people along to share in this breakthrough with me. Coincidentally, my church was having a breakthrough conference in which a few world-renowned speakers and teachers of the Word of God were going to come and deliver a message. I do not think that I did anything wrong or was illogical in my reasoning or thinking, but you can be the judge of that. I sent an email to people that I knew, and it read as follows:

> I would like to invite you all to my church for the 2008 Breakthrough Conference. Tonight and tomorrow night at 7 p.m. we have the honor of listening to two dynamic speakers/communicators/teachers/Men of God preach the Word of God. Their messages will prove to be, at the very least, thought provoking and potentially life

altering. Your current situation—physical, spiritual, emotional, mental, and/or financial does not define you. It is just that—your current situation and can and will change for the better if you want it to and allow God to guide your footsteps. This was the point of last night's message and similar messages will probably be delivered tonight and tomorrow—hence the term Breakthrough Conference. If you aren't interested, but know someone who might be, please pass the message along to them as well. You will not be disappointed in the message or the messenger. I hope to see you there.

Now, I would have understood someone saying something to me had I sent the message to the entire organization. I didn't. I sent it to a select group of individuals. I really did not even expect anyone to respond to the invitation, but I knew that I was supposed to invite them. The VP called me into his office and said, "So an email you sent about some church function is down at HR." I told him I knew it was in HR because I also invited the VP of that department as well. She had invited me to all types of functions via email, or through in-person conversation, so I did not think it to be heresy for me to reciprocate. He proceeded to tell me that I was going to have to go down to HR to discuss the issue. I almost got fired but caught myself before I made any sort of intractable statement. I calmly advised him that I had no problem defending certain things, but an invitation to church was not one of them. I told him that if it was okay for coworkers to invite me to clubs, bars, strip clubs, etc., without any fear of retribution, why should I be required to defend an email inviting people to church? I told him that was not an option and to handle the situation however he saw fit. I did not yell. I simply stood firm on something I deemed important.

The only person in the entire organization that I was willing to talk to about was the VP of HR because we had already had several conversations, some not work-related, in the past. I was actually hoping that the organization tried to get me in trouble because I had people already lined up to help me including lawyers, NAACP members, pastors, and politicians. I wanted war, and for that reason alone, it did not happen. I could already see the CNN headline: "African-American male, former Notre Dame Student athlete, and holder of advanced-level degrees harassed at work for a simple invitation to church." It would have been a complete fiasco, and I was ready and willing to stand right in the middle and fight that battle. Nothing happened. I received a simple phone call from the VP of HR saying, "I know your intentions were good and people email each other all the time to join them in different activities, but please try to stay away from any more church-like invitations, as it always seems to cause an uproar."

I did not agree with it and still do not agree with it but, cool, issue solved.

I sincerely could not believe that someone had the audacity to even think that I would defend my religious beliefs. The lack of education and borderline prejudicial behaviors that I witnessed and that were being perpetuated throughout the organization baffled me. On 9/12/2001, the day after the 9/11 attacks, the phrase "In God We Trust" inundated the airwaves. Signs, TV commercials, radio spots, magazine covers, tattoos, etc., all said the same thing. Times were hard, people were emotionally distraught, and the entire world was looking for a Savior to make it all better. How quickly things changed.

A few years later, The Ten Commandments were removed from courthouses and schools, discussions pertaining to removing the word *God* from the Pledge of Allegiance were rampant, and I even read once on the Internet that people were actually talking about removing the words, "In God We Trust" off money. Wow. And we wonder why the world is the way it is. We are confused as to why wars are waged, murderous rampages take place on an almost regular basis, children die at an alarming rate, and economic turmoil ensues. It is because God is no longer the captain of the team, He is no longer the object of our affection, and He is oftentimes an afterthought. What we are currently experiencing is all because of the world's unwillingness to submit to a higher power.

Sorry, I digress. After dealing with the church incident, it was clear to me that I was not a good fit for the organization. Our values were in complete disarray. I valued education; they did not. I valued religion; they did not. I valued personal and professional growth while the organization seemed unconcerned. I felt that a high level of ethics and moral standards should be consistent throughout the organization and also consistent in one's personal life. The organization had a different mentality, and it was not "practice what you preach." It was more along the lines of "do as I say and not as I do."

In one last effort to see if I was at all valued by the company, particularly the bosses in my functional unit, I wrote up another proposal. This time, I did not even ask for money. I simply asked for a title change that was commensurate with my daily activities. The director advised that she thought it was a good idea and I should present it to the VP. Maybe she thought she was setting me up for failure, but I asked anyway. The VP told me that he considered me to be an assistant director anyway, and when the economy got a little better, he would make the title change official and give me a salary increase.

A few days later, the director told me that the VP asked her why I kept presenting him with proposals and why I always wanted everything in writing. He was by far one of the most self-conscious people I have ever had the misfortune of meeting. He was scared to make a decision and incompetent. He had so little of a backbone that instead of the "powers that be" promoting him to a senior vice president position, an outsider who had a reputation for being controversial and making decisions in the heat of the moment was brought on board. His "skate by and not rock the boat" mentality locked him in to his current position with no room for professional growth outside of switching departments or leaving the company. He probably did not care, but I definitely did. The fact that he was now locked into his position meant that I was locked into mine. Our director was supposed to get promoted to an executive director position, and I was supposed to get promoted to a director position. No such luck. To add insult to injury, the VP acted as if he did not even care. I was perplexed, to say the least.

I did not ask for myself alone, I also asked for the director and the director's assistant to have their titles changed as well. It was a genuine attempt to give us more professional responsibilities within the organization and also add to our credibility as marketing executives. We all kept getting the same excuse: "When the economy turn around, we will take care of you. Just keep working hard, and your efforts will not go unnoticed...I promise." If I had severe mental deficiencies, I might have believed such nonsense. The fact that I oftentimes use more than 1.5 percent of my brain means that I can easily recognize bull**** when I see and/or hear it. Oh well, I prayed about it, stayed in my lane, and kept moving forward.

While I am always ready to deal with non-optimal situations, I am quite the optimist and always hope/plan for the best. To think negative thoughts, in my opinion, breeds negative actions, and those negative actions lead to negative habits. I also believe that if I think positive thoughts, speak in positive affirmations, and believe that it will happen, the universe will conspire to help me and turn those visions into reality. Life throws enough curve balls at us as it is, so to start the game in the negatives does not make any sense to me. I was minding my own business, working hard, and having fun when I heard hints that there were going to be mass layoffs within the organization or people were going to be forced to take salary reductions. I was not thrilled to hear either one. *Oh well, no need to worry,* I thought.

The next day on the news, I heard that all employees within the organization were going to have to take pay cuts in order to avoid layoffs. All salaried employees were to take 10 percent to 15 percent salary reductions, depending on their salary level, and all hourly employees would be cut back from forty hours per week to thirty-two hours per week. Look on the bright side, right? All I had to take was a 10 percent reduction. That equaled to $5,000 less dollars a year.

Anyway, I was *extremely annoyed*. I could not believe that people who made as little money as I was making were hit by this as well. Executive management did a terrible job in allocating, or reallocating, where money should go and from whom it should be taken. Management, in their infinite wisdom, should have the foresight and insight to implement cost-cutting initiatives that would have not had any effect on people making less than $100,000 per year. Prior in-depth analysis before making such drastic changes would have made too much sense, I guess.

Even though I had some level of comfort in the fact that I was not singled out in this situation and everyone was forced to take a pay cut, I was still mad about it. Well, not really mad, because there was nothing I could do about it, but I was still annoyed. I kept hearing people say, "Well, we should all be lucky that we still have jobs."

Many of those people were unskilled, non-hustlin', unable-to-grind types. They felt as if they would be unable to secure employment at another organization. I, on the other hand, felt that I could find another job. Not that it would be easy, but I would have never considered myself stuck.

The next part of this story is quite comical. A few days after the meeting, about six of us were called into the executive offices for a meeting. I was somewhat confused as to why I was on this meeting request, considering all of the other individuals on the invite list were assistants. I listened to the VP talk in this meeting as he proceeded to tell us everything that we had already saw on TV or read on the Internet. He then went on to say that he wanted us all to help out more.

(Side note: they had just cut our pay, and now they were asking us to work more hours.) I am not a mathematician, but that did not make sense to me.

We were all advised that we should help out in booking more reservations, changing the addresses on bad mail envelopes so that the most current addresses would show up in the computer systems, and recycling the old envelopes once we were complete. They, for all intents and purposes, were trying to turn me into a secretary. I sat quietly in the meeting as others asked questions about when the economy would get better and blah blah blah. What made them think that I would actually participate in such nonsense, especially after they cut my salary? I continued to do my normal duties, but participate in the other recommended activities... I did not. The assistants did it for a few days but they, too, quit after they realized there was no point to it. Every time an email would come out asking for assistance with "bad mail," I deleted it. I figured if the two directors and the VPs who were in the meeting were not going to participate in the effort of helping to make the organization better, then why should I? I simply followed their lead.

The days would go by, and I still felt as if my every move was being scrutinized. I could feel the hostility, but I continued to go to work and be as happy and calm as I could be. I tried to stay as engaged as possible, but it was sometimes hard because business was not at its highest level. I had a sense that things within the organization were not going well. There was constant bickering between management and employees, and the idea of teamwork was nonexistent. I tried to maintain a high level of optimism, however. I continued to deal with the people in my department on a daily basis and worked diligently to develop and execute plans that would lead to enhanced revenues within the department.

In the book *The Secret*, the laws of attraction are a focal point. As I have previously mentioned, I live by these rules and, as Rhonda Byrnes notes, they are as irrefutable as the laws of gravity. I began to talk about leaving the casino so much that it began to dominate my thoughts. I was planning what I was going to say when I quit, how I was going to say it, the time of day, what I was going to wear, etc. I paid an exorbitant amount of money to have my résumé and cover letter professionally written and began contacting people whom I felt could rescue me from a situation in which envy, insecurity, inability and unwillingness to act, and fear were rampant. I thought about it, I prayed about it, I talked to family and friends about it, I wrote about it, I dreamed about it, and even asked my two dogs if they were ready to move (they did not answer me). I would go to church, and every message spoken came across as if a big breakthrough was about to come for me. I would get excited every day thinking about the possibility of me leaving the casino world and moving on to bigger and better things. I had gotten used to working under such scrutinizing and hostile conditions. I was so used to it that I began to feel as if it was normal because when the bosses started acting too nicely, I thought something was wrong. My intuitions were right, and they usually are. The unusual niceness, if I can use that word, was so extreme that I knew a storm was brewing and heading my way. It was the calm before the storm.

I remember the incident like it was yesterday. I was working in the casino host office when the VP called and said, "Hey, can you come upstairs for a minute?"

I figured he wanted to ask me something about one of the budgets I had recently put together for a national marketing promotion aimed at augmenting business and increasing incremental revenue. I walked upstairs and saw a friend of mine sitting in the boss's office; I still did not think anything was wrong. It's crazy how my heart has started beating fast again as I relive the incident.

Anyway, I just thought she was there to say hi since I had not seen her in quite some time. I sat down in the chair and, as usual, asked everyone how they were doing. They both responded agreeably. I then said, "What's going on?"

Before I even finished the sentence, my friend, the employment assistant manager, sat all the way up in her chair and said, "Charles, you know me and..."

I zoned out because I knew what was about to happen. She proceeded to tell me that the hotel/casino was undergoing a management restructure and many "non-essential" manager- and director-level positions were being eliminated. After all the harassment, envy, trite remarks, tension, scrutiny, and undue treatment that I endured, this was the thanks I got. I worked my a** off every day. I wrote all of the promotional letters, I did all of the budgets for our specific group's promotional events, I did the monthly commission checks so that people could get paid in a timely manner for their hard work. I worked to make our group an actual team that worked together and cared for the welfare and well-being of another. The worst part was that the girl whom I had developed a close working relationship with, the one to whom I reported, did not even have the courage to show up. She decided it was more important to attend a meeting. But like I have said before, we were all nothing but puppets for the company.

The employment assistant manager and VP went on to tell me that the separation had nothing to do with my performance because I was doing a good job and that it was nothing more than a business decision. She then pulled out a bunch of papers for me to read and sign. Signing that severance package would have ruined me. Within the document was an exhaustive list of things that I could not do—write a book was one of them. The real deal breaker was that they offered me $3800 as an offer to not do anything drastic such as sue or talk negatively about the organization or its employees. She advised that a notary had to be there to legitimize my signature and also noted that the organization would not contest me immediately filing for unemployment.

I was in such a state of shock because I was completed blindsided. I could not help but think and say they did me a major disservice by bringing me there. I had accepted an unacceptable salary, I had defended situations that others would have never defended, and I had handled the adversity with grace and poise. There was no management restructuring; I just think that the economic downturn gave them a reason to get rid of the lone black kid on the block. I had already heard a few days before my separation that the hotel/casino was in the process of hiring two more management/director-level employees. I saw how they doctored a termination letter to one of our independent agents just one month prior, so I knew that they were doing the same thing to me. The feelings of betrayal, misguidance, and anger were all there. The only way I knew how to handle them and keep my cool was to stay calm and quiet. I prayed for strength as the VP and employment assistant manager were talking to me. Even now I am at a loss for words. All I knew at that particular moment was that it would be foolish of me to accept the severance agreement and sign the package without first speaking to an employment lawyer about my situation. So that is what I did.

I went in, told him my story, and he was appalled at my level of pay and the way I was treated. We decided the case was worth pursuing, so that is what we decided to do. Every action is met with an equal and opposite reaction. So there I was—well-educated, well-travelled, well-written, optimistic, and jobless. What was I to do? It was a mystery at that point, but I knew that I had to hand all of my fears and worries over to God. He sent His Son to die for me so that I would not have to bear such burdens. What would happen next? Only God knew, and only time would tell. As I have said before, the only way to reasonably predict the future is to invent it, and that was exactly what I planned to do.

GOD FAVORS THE FAITHFUL

As long as I breathe, there is hope. As long as I remain faithful and believe that God's promises are "yes" and "Amen," I can move forward with a resolute will and spirit of determination. All I have to do is what I can, and when I cannot do anymore, God—the grand architect of the universe—will do the rest. This is what I told myself everyday as I networked with people, sent massive amounts of emails, submitted résumés, interviewed for jobs, and tried to remain focused. I was on a rollercoaster, and I was on one of the down slopes. Fortunately, I knew that nothing stays the same...not for long, anyway.

I was fine for the first couple of months. I felt it was a mini-vacation. I was able to work out more, spend more time with friends, work on me, and relax. I was studying for the LSAT anyway, so it was a welcomed relief from the monotony associated with going to work every day. Not having a job ensured that my financial situation was not optimal. Again, God favored me and put people into my path that were willing to help me. My girlfriend would buy groceries for the house, family members would help me pay rent, and a few friends donated to my cause as well, just to help me in my time of need. All of their assistance was greatly appreciated, and I am forever thankful. It proved to be most difficult to make ends meet on a $350 per week unemployment check. Inconsistent odd jobs and sporadic part-time work helped a little bit, but that earned money was nothing of significance.

Although I had a few weak moments in which I questioned God and the purpose for my journey, I knew that I had to remain faithful. I knew that God placed all people in a predetermined location at a predetermined time to learn something, help others, or be helped. I wasn't sure what was going on with me, but I did know that I had no other choice but to lean on God and pray that He would carry me through. Times were hard, though. For approximately six months, I had no money and had to rely on the hospitality and willingness of others to help.

Despite my level of faith, the devil is strong and tries his best to infiltrate the minds of people in a vulnerable state. I was there, and for a minute or two, he almost had me. I actually contemplated entering the homes of others to find food and money while they were not home. As a result of me being home every day, I knew the comings and goings of mostly everyone on my street. I had no intentions of hurting anyone, but I knew I had to survive. I was eating one meal a day and had to take care of my dogs as well. At least they were still eating good. Neglecting them was not an option in my mind. I planned, plotted, and strategized to the point that making a mistake was slim to none. I knew which doors were unlocked, which windows were open, and who else was in the neighborhood during the day who could have potentially spotted me. I felt as if I was at war with the world. Federal government agencies had contacted me about potential career opportunities, but the process was taking an extremely long time. I was almost out of options, or so I thought. I did not want to engage in such acts, but survival thinking had taking over. I continued to pray.

As I was driving to an FBI-testing procedure one day, a voice in my head said, "Today is the day." In my mind, that statement meant that it was time to fulfill my plan. It was foolproof. I knew where I was going, what time, what house, what door, etc. I was not gambling; this was science. I had $9.82 in the bank and had accumulated approximately $40K in credit card debt as a result of not having enough real money to live and pay bills. What choice did I have? Probably one million other choices, but I was blind to them all at that point. I continued to pray. I had to remain faithful. God takes care of the birds, so I knew He would take care of me. He said He would, so I had no choice but to believe it.

After testing was over, my mind went back to the "plan." When I started the car to go home, I received a phone call from an individual within a federal government contracting organization. The voice on the other end said, "Sorry for the delay, everything is confirmed, we will be sending you quite the handsome offer letter today."

I sat in the car and cried. God does favor the faithful. While I knew that I still had to pay bills, I no longer had to choose between paying a bill, getting gas, or buying food. I could do it all and more. I could send money to my mom, I could go out to eat, and I could have fun...well, more fun than usual. I remained faithful. I was bold in my requests, and my wishes were granted.

I needed faith, desire, resilience, and patience. I am glad that I didn't do anything stupid. There are dichotomies in life: good vs. evil, right vs. wrong, day vs. night, love vs. hate. It is up to us to choose how we respond to life situations. As long as I breathe, there is hope. Scars remind us that the past is real. Even though I was once again fighting an internal battle and losing, my Savior intervened and said enough is enough. Believe me when I tell you: God does favor the faithful.

THE PROPHECY

It is oftentimes hard to stand in a tunnel, not see the light, and have the intestinal fortitude to move forward. It is imperative, however, to only speak positive affirmations into one's life and proceed with a resolute will and unshakeable determination to succeed. While I was somewhat similar to the millions of other people who had found themselves out of gainful employment and had no clear direction of what would happen, I believed and still believe in a God that gives me the strength to walk by faith and not by sight. Ephesians 4:29 says, "Let no foul speech come out of your mouth, but only such as will build up where it is necessary, so as to add a blessing to the listeners." I believe that by not succumbing to negative thoughts and speaking what I hope for, wish for, and pray for, God will open the gates of heaven so that I can be a blessing to others. At this point in my life, I have to remain positive. I have a wonderful fiancée and a beautiful little girl. They are smart, fun, confident, supportive, beautiful, and believe in me. They make me want to do better and make the challenges in my life much easier to handle. Did my girls come into my life for a reason? The answer is yes. Will they stay for a season or a lifetime? Let's speak prophetically and say a lifetime. Only God knows.

Not a day goes by that these words are not spoken: "Life is what you make it, at least that's what they say. Well, I think I am going to make it and fulfill my dreams someday. I feel this fire growing deep inside of me. I am so inspired knowing that it is my destiny. I breathe like a champion; I speak I am a champion,

I dream I am a champion... it is meant to be. My will is getting stronger, I cannot wait any longer—I am speaking these words that are inside of me because I am a believer. I know that I can make it, no matter what they say. I am a believer. The future is now, and it starts today." These words resonate so deeply within me that I would do a disservice to myself if I did not believe in the power that they hold. God has given me many gifts, and He expects that I use them to the best of my ability.

Dennis Kimbro once stated, "Life seems to have been designed so that every man who achieves great success must first undergo a testing period—sometimes many of them—through which he is tested for courage, faith, endurance, and the capacity to overcome." As I have spoken of on several occasions in this book, my level of resiliency is unparalleled, not because of my doing, but because of God's grace and mercy. He has climbed mountains, weathered storms, fought battles, jumped hurdles, and swam against the strongest currents with me on His back because He knew that I was unable to face such trials and tribulations alone. Because of what He has done for me, I have a newfound strength to face the world and use the skills and knowledge He has given me to the best of my abilities.

I have been blessed by the almighty to speak life into situations that seem dead. He has given me a spirit of discernment to know when things are not progressing as they should, and before I go on with the remainder of this final chapter, I must speak life back into my hometown of Flint, Michigan. To all my fellow Flint-Stones, I speak these words with an absolute level of sincerity and a heavy heart because I know that we were all designed to do more. I implore you to look deep within yourself and figure out what you can do, as a child of the Most High God, to make your corner of the world better. Be the change that you want to see.

> Courage is not the absence of fear or doubt; it is the ability to act in spite of them. Any coward can hide behind a

mask and a gun. It takes courage to settle your differences through words and understanding. As you are all aware, murders in Flint take place almost as often as dogs bark. It has become a sad fact of life that it happens so often that it does not even seem to have a major impact on the way we view societal norms and violence as a whole. Young black men need to stand up and choose not to be victims of the circumstances. All too often, it has been said that we do not have a choice, when the fact of the matter is, we do have a choice. We all have a choice to learn how to become successful in the world or become a menace to society. We wonder why, as a group of individuals, we never make it to prominent positions in this world. No one even considers the notion that white America does not believe in us because we do not believe in ourselves. Every time we try to take two steps forward, a tragedy occurs that catapults us ten steps back. It has been said that, "For of those to whom much is given, much is required." As a result of being given certain unalienable rights, by God, such as life, liberty and the pursuit of happiness, it is our obligation to do what is right not only for ourselves, but also for our fellow citizens and those who worked so hard to pave the way for us. To continue to remain boxed in and not work tirelessly to transcend any and all negative stereotypes would be uncivilized. We are not barbarians; we are not caged animals who upon release attack any and everything within its sight; we are not uneducated thugs who don't know any better; we are Sons and Daughters of the King of kings, The Lord of lords—Heirs to the throne of grace, mercy, and righteousness. Do not let anyone tell you or convince you otherwise.

Young black men senselessly killing other young black men. That was not God's intention when he created us. The ultimate goal is for us all to love one another. If we continue to kill each other, sooner or later, there will be no one left. We are all running the same race, so it is counterproductive for us to trip each other up. There are enough pressures placed on us simply because we are young and black. We do not need the added pressure of wondering when and if one of our "own" is going to try to send us to the grave before it is truly our time. Successful young black men, loving fathers, concerned neighbors, or menaces to society...

Those are our options. We were all sent here to fulfill a Divine purpose. It is different for each person and because of that, I cannot directly comment on what it is. I can tell you, however, that it is not killing people just for fun.

Rest assured that during our short stay on this planet, we will have an impact on the lives of others. Whether or not that impact is positive or negative is your decision. I pray for all of the men and women who read this... take it to heart and make your own destiny. Do not be a menace to society or a victim of the circumstances. Be an inspiration to others and the Disciple that God meant for you to become. Stand up. Take your places. We are keepers of our own legacy. Never forget that God is a forgiving God. Regardless of your current situation, it can be changed. Remain strong and pray that on judgment day you hear the nine most important words you will ever hear in your life: "Well done, my good and faithful servant, well done."

I have come to a point in my life in which I am comfortable with the person that God has made. I believe in me, not because others believe in me, but because I know that the Creator does not make mistakes. While I recognize that sometimes things in life are hard to digest, I also understand that without struggle, there is no progress. I do not know what the future holds, but I can tell you this: success is right around the corner. When I say success, do not automatically assume that I am speaking of financial success. While that is important, the success I speak of goes much deeper than that. The success of which I dream includes having a loving wife and kids, having a strong relationship with my parents, sister, and other family members. Success means being a father and not just a "baby daddy." Success means working diligently to expand God's kingdom. Success means doing what is right when no one is looking. Success means opening doors for people who cannot do it themselves. Success means talking to kids about a life without fear, without shame, without doubt, without regret, and without hatred. Success means teaching, speaking, living, and learning in such a way that I leave an indelible mark on the hearts and minds of every single individual that I encounter. Success means speaking truisms if it is necessary to enhance the life of another. Success means not being afraid to tell others about my God and what He did for me when He sent His Son to die on the cross so that my sins could be forgiven. Success means waking up every morning and saying, "Thank you for allowing me to see another day."

As I look back on what I have accomplished so far and reflect on how God has been there with me all along, I cannot help but be excited about what the future holds. A good friend read the following quote to me. I don't know who said it, but it is as follows.

"A wise man once said that you can have anything in life, if you are willing to sacrifice everything else for it. What he meant is nothing comes without a price. So before you go into battle, you better decide how much you are willing to lose. Too often, going after what feels good means letting go of what you know is right. Letting someone in can mean abandoning the walls you've spent a lifetime building. Of course, the toughest sacrifices are the ones we don't see coming. There is no time to come up with a strategy, to pick a side or to measure the potential loss. When that happens, when the battle chooses us and not the other way around, that's when the sacrifice can turn out to be more than we can bear. How sweet it is, that when all is said and done, we realize that we could not only bear more than we thought, but we also claimed the victory. The most divine future will always depend upon the necessity and ability to surrender the past..."

While the last few years of my life have been quite turbulent and the money did not add up the way I would have liked it to, I can say with an unwavering spirit of truth that the experiences gained were priceless. While I recognize the fact that there is no blueprint for me to follow, I have come to a place in my life in which I can listen to my heart and let it guide me. A successful author, international speaker, and doctoral degree holder are my next goals in life.

Some people want to be doctors. Some people want to be lawyers. Some of us, however, want to change a nation. Will I achieve everything that my heart, mind, and soul desires? If it is the Lord's will...I absolutely will. If He has other plans for me, then so be it. He leads, and I follow. I mentioned it earlier in this book, and I will say it again: Proverbs 3:5-6 says, "Trust in the Lord with all your heart and lean not unto your own understanding. In all your ways acknowledge him and He will direct your paths." While I have allowed some temptations to knock me off of my path in the past, I am only human, and mistakes are inevitable. I cannot and will not be afraid to move forward and face those challenges head-on because the Bible says that God has not given us the spirit of fear, but of power and of love and of sound mind. I take His teachings as absolute truth and know that there is no mountain too tall, no hurdle too high, no storm too strong, no waters too deep to successfully navigate as long as I keep my eyes on God. I know it may not be easy all of the time, but I also know and recognize that whomsoever God guides, no one can lead astray. I realize that in this life, I might have to give up some things that I cannot keep to gain something that I can never lose. Let me be explicit: by gaining something I can never lose, I am speaking of God's grace, God's mercy, and my eternal salvation. It is my wish that you gain the same.

Michael Jordan said it best, and I will recapture it in all of its essence right now:

SCARS, EXILE, AND VINDICATION

Look me in the eye. It is okay that you are scared. So am I. But we are scared for different reasons. I am scared of what I won't become, you're scared of what I could become. Look at me. I will not let myself end where I started. I will not let myself finish where I began. I know what is within me, even if you cannot see it yet. Look me in the eyes. I have something more important than courage—I have patience. I will become what I know I am—legendary...